TIME MANAGEMENT
ADVENTURES
A Kid's Guide to Mastering Time

Revised & Extended: Second Edition

Part of the Skillful Adventures™ Series
With The Friends and The Professor

Dr. Joy Chacko

Originally published in 2023 by Joy Chacko, PhD

Revised & Extended: Second Edition, 2025

ISBN: 979-8-9934027-1-0

Publisher: Joy Chacko, PhD · Skillful Adventures™ Series

SkillfulAdventures.com

Disclaimer

This book is for educational purposes only. While every effort has been made to ensure accuracy, the author and publisher assume no responsibility for errors, omissions, or outcomes resulting from the use of the information contained herein.

Featuring Comprehensive Time Management Toolkits, Summary Charts, a Self-Assessment Quiz, and Results to Help Children Excel in Daily Life. These resources complement the time management concepts and principles woven into a delightful story narrated by The Friends and The Professor.

✿ Skillful Adventures™ Series ✿

Stories Kids Love. Skills They Keep for Life.

✓ Time Management

✓ Project Management

✓ Mini-CFO Adventures

✓ Leadership — and More Coming Soon!

✸ Visit **SkillfulAdventures.com**

Table of Contents

Overview

Sincerely,
Joy Chacko, PhD.
Author, Researcher, and Educator

Part 1:

Foundations of Time Management

Master the essential principles to build a strong time management foundation! These chapters introduce the key building blocks of managing time effectively.

Chapter 1

The Time Management Adventure Begins

In This Chapter: Meet our time heroes—Timmy the Tortoise, Bella the Bunny, Max the Monkey, and Lily the Ladybug—along with their wise guide, the old owl Professor Timekeeper, as they embark on an exciting journey to master time management.

Word to Remember: Prioritization

Once upon a time, in the lively and charming town of **Clocksville**, four best friends were excited about their latest big idea: building the best treehouse anyone had ever seen.

- **Timmy the Tortoise** was calm and steady, always taking his time to think before he acted.

- **Bella the Bunny** was quick and full of energy, often hopping from one activity to another.

- **Max the Monkey** was clever and curious, always looking for the next fun thing to do.

- **Lily the Ladybug** was organized and thoughtful, with a love for making lists and helping her friends.

They had gathered wood, nails, and tools during their summer vacation, determined to turn their dream into reality. But despite their excitement and hard work, the project didn't go as planned.

The Unfinished Treehouse: Will They Finish It This Vacation?

"Hold this steady!" Max shouted as he tried to hammer two boards together.

"I can't!" Bella replied, hopping from one side of the tree to the other. "I need to finish painting the sign first!"

Timmy moved slowly, carefully measuring the wood, but he hadn't even started cutting it yet.

Meanwhile, Lily was busy making a long list of tasks, but no one seemed to follow it.

By the end of the day, the friends were surrounded by scattered boards, tools, and half-done tasks. The treehouse looked more like a wobbling pile of sticks than the amazing fort they had imagined.

Frustrated, they all sat down under a shady tree nearby.

"Why can't we finish anything?" Max asked, scratching his head.

"Last summer, we ran out of time," Bella said with a sigh. "And now it feels like it's happening all over again this vacation."

"We've dreamed about this treehouse for so long," Max said, his tail flicking with determination. "I really want to make it happen this time!"

"Maybe we're just not good at building treehouses," Lily said, her wings drooping.

"That's not true," said a deep, kind voice.

Meeting Professor Timekeeper

The friends looked up to see **Professor Timekeeper**, the wise old owl, perched on a low branch above them.

"Hello, my young adventurers," he said with a friendly smile. "I've been watching you, and I think I know what the problem is. Would you like to learn the secret to making the most of your time?"

The friends exchanged excited glances and shouted together, "Yes, please!"

Professor Timekeeper flapped his wings and perched closer. "The secret is something called **time management**. Think of it as a magical map that helps you plan your day. It shows you what's most important and how to make time for everything that matters."

"Wow! A magical map?" Bella's ears twitched with excitement.

"Exactly!" the Professor said, nodding. "But to use it, you need to learn a very important word: **Prioritization**. It means figuring out what's most important and doing that first."

Professor Timekeeper smiled knowingly. "By the end of our adventure, I'll also share some special tools that can help you stay organized and make the most of your time."

The Start of an Adventure

Lily's eyes lit up. "So, if we learn time management, we can finally finish our treehouse?"

Professor Timekeeper nodded. "Absolutely. By the end of our adventure, you'll know how to manage your time like true time heroes. Besides, strong time management is a critical skill for success in life."

Professor Timekeeper paused for a moment, his wise eyes twinkling. "*The world is truly wonderful, and together, we can make it even more so. Time management is one of the essential tools that helps us achieve that. Everything in life—humans, animals, trees, flowers, and even the stars above—grows and evolves with time. By managing our time wisely, we can nurture what matters most and make every moment count.*"

The friends listened intently; their excitement renewed. They were ready to embark on this adventure with fresh determination and the guidance of their wise Professor.

Timmy smiled. "I can't wait to start!"

"Me neither!" Max said, jumping up.

"Let's go!" Bella added, hopping in excitement.

Professor Timekeeper spread his wings. "Then follow me. Our first stop is learning how to **prioritize**!"

And so, the adventure began, with Timmy, Bella, Max, Lily, and their guide, Professor Timekeeper, ready to unlock the secrets of time management and turn their dream treehouse into a reality.

For Parents and Teachers: Key Takeaways from Chapter 1

1. **Prioritization**: Children learn that some tasks are more important than others, and starting with those helps them make the most of their time.

2. **Introduction of Characters**: Kids get to know Timmy, Bella, Max, Lily, and Professor Timekeeper, who will guide them on their time management journey.

3. **Engaging Tone**: The story introduces time management as a fun and magical concept that applies to real-world challenges, like building a treehouse.

Time-Mastery Tools: Empowering All Ages

A Note for Readers

These adaptable tools provide **valuable insights** for all ages, from *playful learning* for kids to *practical strate*gies for adults. This book serves as a **comprehensive reference** and a timely reminder that readers can revisit throughout their lives, offering a **toolkit for effective time management**.

These tools are not just for kids; they are strategies used by students and professionals alike to excel in daily life. You'll find suggestions in relevant chapters on which tools parents and teachers may explore to reinforce lessons.

Research shows that **time management is a critical skill for success**, yet many struggle to find enough time for their most important tasks. By reviewing or using these tools with children, parents and teachers can gain insights into time management while helping instill this essential skill early on.

Introduced in a fun and engaging manner, these concepts aim to create lasting impressions. When explored together, they provide a **strong foundation for lifelong time management skills**.

Key Tools for Chapter 1:

- **Big Rock Exercise:** Helps children identify their most important tasks ("Big Rocks") and prioritize completing them first.

- **My 24-Hour Time Tracking Chart:** A fun and interactive way for kids to analyze their time usage and identify areas for improvement.

- **Blank Prioritization Table:** A hands-on tool for kids to list and rank their daily tasks by importance.

Chapter 2

Setting Priorities:
The Treasure Map of Time

In This Chapter: Join Timmy, Bella, Max, Lily, and Professor Timekeeper as they uncover the secret of setting priorities using a magical treasure map. Learn how focusing on the most important tasks first can help you achieve your goals and make the most of your time.

Word to Remember: Prioritize

The friends were back under the shady tree, still brainstorming ways to make their dream treehouse a reality. Pieces of wood, nails, paint, ropes, and tools were scattered around them, but it felt like no progress had been made. "Where do we even start?" Timmy asked, looking at the unfinished treehouse.

Max scratched his head. "We tried building the ladder, but then we got distracted painting the walls. And don't even get me started on the roof!"

"I keep making lists, but we never finish the first task before moving to the next one," Lily said with a sigh.

Bella's ears twitched. "It feels like we're chasing everything at once and getting nowhere."

Professor Timekeeper, perched nearby, smiled warmly. "It sounds like you need a **plan** to help you focus on the most important tasks first. Let me show you something magical."

He pulled out an old, rolled-up map from under his wing and spread it out on the ground.

"Wow!" Max exclaimed. "A treasure map?"

Professor Timekeeper nodded. "Indeed! But this is no ordinary map. It's a **Treasure Map of Time**, and it teaches an important lesson about setting priorities."

Discovering the Treasure Map of Time

The friends leaned in closer. The map was covered with drawings of treasures, each marked in **red**, **yellow**, or **blue**.

"**Setting priorities is like searching for treasure**," Professor Timekeeper explained. "You must focus on the most valuable treasures first. These are marked in red, representing your most important tasks. Yellow treasures are less important, and blue treasures can wait until the end."

Lily's eyes lit up. "So, we should start with the red tasks—like building the ladder—before moving on to the others?"

"Exactly!" said the Professor. "By focusing on what matters most, you'll make better use of your time and avoid getting stuck."

The friends decided to give it a try. They used the map to identify their "red treasures" for the treehouse project:

- **Build the ladder** so they could safely climb into the treehouse.
- **Secure the base** to make the structure sturdy.

The yellow treasures included painting the walls and decorating the interior, while the blue treasures, like adding curtains and flower boxes, could wait until the end.

Putting Prioritization into Action

With their priorities set, the friends got to work. Timmy measured the wood for the ladder while Bella fetched nails and tools. Max hammered the pieces together, and Lily checked the plans to keep them on track.

Step by step, the ladder took shape. When it was finished, they all cheered.

"This is so much easier now that we're focusing on one thing at a time!" Bella said, hopping with excitement.

After securing the base, the friends moved on to painting the walls. By the end of the day, their treehouse began to take shape, inching closer to the fort they had always imagined.

Professor Timekeeper beamed with pride. "Well done, my young adventurers! You've mastered the art of prioritization. Remember, always focus on the most important tasks first. It will help you achieve your goals and make the most of your time."

The friends nodded, feeling proud and excited to use their new skill in all their future adventures.

For Parents and Teachers: Key Takeaways from Chapter 2

1. **Building on Prioritization**: While Chapter 1 introduced the concept of prioritization, this chapter dives deeper into its practical application. Using the Treasure Map of Time, children learn how to identify and focus on their most important tasks.

2. **Practical Visualization**: The use of colors (red, yellow, blue) helps children visualize task importance and understand how prioritization works.

3. **Relatable Example**: Connecting the treasure map to the treehouse project demonstrates how prioritization helps tackle real-world challenges.

Tools to Support Learning for Chapter 2

To help children understand and practice the concept of setting priorities, parents and teachers may find these tools helpful:

- **Blank Prioritization Table**: A simple tool for kids to list their tasks and group them into red, yellow, and blue categories, just like the treasures on the map.

- **Big Rock Exercise**: Encourages children to identify their "big rocks" (the most important tasks) and focus on completing these first.

- **My 24-Hour Time Tracking Chart**: Helps kids reflect on how they spend their time and identify opportunities to prioritize their most valuable "treasures."

Chapter 3

**Creating Routines:
The Magic of Daily Rituals**

In This Chapter: Discover the magic of creating daily routines with Timmy, Bella, Max, Lily, and Professor Timekeeper. Learn how daily rituals can bring structure, joy, and success to your day.

Word to Remember: Routines

The treehouse project was coming along, but the friends quickly realized something was still slowing them down.

"We keep running out of time to finish everything!" Bella said, frustrated, as she set down her paintbrush.

"It feels like we're all over the place," Timmy added, looking at the scattered tools and half-finished tasks.

Professor Timekeeper nodded thoughtfully. "That's because you're working without a **routine**. Let's take a little walk—I want to show you something."

The friends followed the Professor through a winding forest trail. Soon, they reached a small clearing, where they discovered a bustling little village. Magical creatures moved with purpose, their tasks perfectly in sync.

The Village of Rituals was unlike any place the friends had ever seen. It was home to magical creatures—gnomes, fairies, and other whimsical enchanted beings—each with their own unique charm. Some had twinkling wings that shimmered in the sunlight, while others had long, pointed ears that perked up as they worked. Dressed in nature-inspired clothing made of leaves, petals, and soft moss, the villagers moved gracefully through their daily tasks. Everywhere they looked, there was a sense of rhythm and harmony, as if the entire village was dancing to the same invisible tune. Laughter filled the air as they watered gardens, prepared meals, and tidied their homes—all while humming cheerful melodies. It was clear that their secret to happiness and success lay in the magic of their daily routines.

"Welcome to the Village of Rituals," said a cheerful gnome, waving from the garden. "We live our lives by following daily routines. These routines help us finish our tasks on time and make space for joy and celebration!"

Learning the Magic of Routines

The friends watched in awe as the villagers worked together seamlessly. Some were watering plants, others were preparing meals, and a few were singing songs while cleaning up. Everyone seemed happy and organized.

Professor Timekeeper smiled. "This is what happens when you create routines—or daily rituals. By doing certain tasks at the same time every day, you form habits that make it easier to reach your goals."

Max tilted his head. "But how do we know what to include in our routine?"

"Start by listing the things you need to do every day," the Professor explained. "Then think about what's most important and when you can do it best. That's how you create your magical routine!"

The friends decided to give it a try. They sat together and wrote down their daily tasks:

- Timmy focused on measuring and cutting wood for the treehouse in the morning when he felt most alert.

- Bella planned her painting sessions in the afternoon, her favorite time to be creative.

- Max made time to organize their tools each evening, so they were ready for the next day.

- Lily created a checklist to track their progress and make sure nothing was forgotten.

The Power of Routines in Action

As they followed their routines each day, something amazing happened. The treehouse started to take shape faster than ever. Tasks that once felt overwhelming now seemed manageable, and they even had time left for games and laughter.

"Wow! Routines really do make a difference!" Bella exclaimed.

The magical creatures of the Village of Rituals noticed their progress and invited the friends to join their evening celebration. They danced under the stars, realizing how routines had brought not only structure but also happiness to their lives.

Professor Timekeeper watched proudly. "Remember, my young adventurers: Routines are like a magical spell. They bring order to your days, help you manage your time, and make room for all the things you love."

The friends cheered, ready to use their new skill to tackle any challenge— starting with finishing their treehouse!

For Parents and Teachers: Key Takeaways from Chapter 3

1. **Concept of Routines**: This chapter introduces children to the importance of creating routines to bring structure and joy to their days.

2. **Practical Application**: By guiding children to list their daily tasks and prioritize them, the story connects routines to better time management.

3. **Engaging Storytelling**: The Village of Rituals and its magical creatures make the concept of routines fun and memorable for kids.

Tools to Support Learning for Chapter 3

To reinforce the concept of creating routines, parents and teachers may find the following tools helpful:

-   **My Weekly Planner Template**: A simple grid to help children plan their weekly activities, including school, homework, and playtime.

-   **Daily Success Reflection Worksheet**: Encourages kids to reflect on their routines at the end of the day:

    o   *What did I do well today?*

    o   *What can I do better tomorrow?*

-   **The "What's My Frog?" Worksheet**: Helps children identify the most important task (the "frog") in their routine and start their day by completing it.

finaL touchES — Roof COMplEtE!

paiNT thE Roof

SECuRE thE paNEls

asSEMblE Roof fRaME

MEasuRE and cut wood

Chapter 4

Breaking Tasks into Smaller Steps: Climbing the Task Mountain

In This Chapter: Follow Timmy, Bella, Max, Lily, and Professor Timekeeper as they tackle the towering Task Mountain. Learn how breaking a big goal into smaller steps makes even the hardest challenges achievable.

Word to Remember: **Steps** (Breaking big tasks into smaller, manageable steps.)

A Daunting Task

The treehouse was finally starting to take shape, but one big challenge loomed ahead: the roof.

"How are we ever going to finish the roof?" Max groaned, staring at the pile of wood and nails. "It's too much work!"

Bella hopped nervously. "And don't forget we still need to make the ladder and paint the walls!"

Timmy, calm as ever, scratched his head. "It's like trying to climb a mountain. Where do we even start?"

Professor Timekeeper perched on a nearby branch and hooted softly. "That's a perfect metaphor, Timmy! Every big task is like climbing a mountain. It looks impossible when you focus on the entire thing. But what if you climb it one small step at a time?"

Professor Timekeeper spread his wings dramatically. "Let me tell you about"

"Task Mountain, a place where adventurers like you learn the secret of tackling big goals. Imagine standing at the base of a towering mountain, its peak hidden in the clouds. What would you do?"

"Run away," Max said, wide-eyed.

"Or take it one step at a time?" Lily suggested thoughtfully.

"Exactly!" said the Professor. "The trick to climbing Task Mountain—or finishing any big task—is to break it into smaller, manageable steps. Focus on one milestone at a time, and you'll reach the top before you know it!"

The friends looked at each other, inspired.

Climbing Task Mountain: One Step at a Time

"Let's try this with our treehouse," the Professor continued. "What's the biggest task you need to finish?"

"The roof!" Max said quickly.

"Great! Now, what's the first step you need to take to start the roof?"

Timmy thought for a moment. "We could measure and cut the wood into the right sizes."

"That's your first milestone," the Professor said. "What comes next?"

"We'll need to nail the pieces together," Bella added.

"And then paint it before attaching it," Lily chimed in.

Professor Timekeeper nodded. "See? By breaking the roof into smaller steps, it doesn't seem so overwhelming anymore."

The friends got to work, focusing on one step at a time. First, they measured and cut the wood. Then they carefully nailed the pieces together, celebrating each milestone they reached. By the end of the day, they had finished the frame of the roof and felt a huge sense of accomplishment.

The Secret of Task Mountain

As the sun set, Professor Timekeeper gathered the friends under the treehouse.

"Remember, my young adventurers," he said, "every big task is just a series of small steps. When you focus on one step at a time, you can climb any mountain—or finish any roof!"

Bella smiled. "It's funny how breaking things down makes them feel less scary."

"And more fun!" Max added.

The friends cheered, ready to tackle the next part of their project with their new strategy.

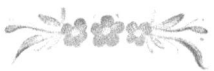

For Parents and Teachers: Key Takeaways from Chapter 4

1. **Concept of Breaking Tasks**: This chapter teaches children how to break large tasks or goals into smaller, manageable steps, using the metaphor of climbing Task Mountain.

2. **Practical Application**: By connecting the concept to the treehouse project, children see how breaking down tasks helps them make progress and stay motivated.

3. **Engaging Storytelling**: The Task Mountain metaphor and the friends' teamwork make the lesson fun and memorable for kids.

Tools to Support Learning for Chapter 4

To reinforce the concept of breaking tasks into smaller steps, parents and teachers may find the following tools helpful:

- **Task Breakdown Worksheet**: A simple template where kids can write a big task and break it into smaller, actionable steps.

- **Progress Tracker**: A visual chart for marking milestones, helping kids see and celebrate their progress.

- **Daily Success Reflection Worksheet**: Prompts like:

  o *What was one big task I broke into smaller steps today?*

  o *What milestone did I reach, and how did I feel?*

Chapter 5

❀✿❀

Using a Calendar or Planner: The Time Management Compass

In This Chapter: Join Timmy, Bella, Max, Lily, and Professor Timekeeper as they discover the Time Management Compass, a magical tool that helps them plan their days and stay organized. Learn how calendars and planners can make life less stressful and more fulfilling.

Word to Remember: Plan

The Mystery Object

It was another busy day in Clocksville, and the friends were back to work on their treehouse. The walls were finally coming together, but the roof and ladder still seemed like a distant dream.

"We keep forgetting what needs to be done," Bella sighed, wiping her brow. "And we're always running out of time!"

"Maybe we need a better plan," Lily suggested, adjusting her list, which was getting longer by the minute.

As they debated what to do next, Max spotted something shiny poking out of the dirt nearby. "What's that?" he asked, racing over to investigate.

It was an unusual compass, but instead of pointing north, south, east, or west, its face displayed dates, tasks, and events.

Professor Timekeeper swooped down from his perch and landed next to them. "Ah, my young adventurers, you've found the **Time Management Compass**! This magical tool helps you plan your days and stay organized, just like a calendar or planner."

"How does it work?" Timmy asked, intrigued.

The Professor held up the compass. "Think of it as your guide to organizing your time. You use it to decide when to work on each task and how much time to spend. By following your plan, you'll stay on track and finish what you start."

"Like planning our treehouse tasks?" Bella asked.

"Exactly," said the Professor. "Let's start by listing everything you still need to do. Then we'll use the compass to schedule time for each task."

Using the Compass to Tackle the Treehouse

The friends eagerly wrote down all their remaining treehouse tasks, among other things:

- Finish building the roof.

- Paint the walls.

- Attach the ladder.

- Add decorations.

- Install safety railings.

- Create a cozy seating area.

- Build a sign for the treehouse.

"Now," Professor Timekeeper continued, "we'll decide which task to work on first and how much time to spend on it. This way, you won't feel overwhelmed, and you'll know exactly what to do next."

The friends decided to work on the roof first, giving it two hours. They scheduled time for painting and attaching the ladder after that, with short breaks in between.

With their plan in place, they got to work. Following the Time Management Compass, they tackled each task in order, staying focused and organized. To their surprise, they finished the roof and had enough time to start painting the walls!

The Magic of Staying Organized

As the sun began to set, the friends gathered under the treehouse to admire their progress.

"Staying organized really helped us get more done," Lily said, her wings fluttering with excitement.

"And it felt less stressful," Timmy added.

"That's the magic of tools like calendars and planners," Professor Timekeeper said with a proud hoot. "When you organize your time, you can achieve your goals and still have time for fun."

The friends cheered, eager to use the Time Management Compass for the rest of their project and share their new skill with others.

For Parents and Teachers: Key Takeaways from Chapter 5

1. **Concept of Organization**: This chapter introduces children to using calendars or planners to organize their time effectively, using the metaphor of the Time Management Compass.

2. **Practical Benefits**: Kids learn how scheduling tasks reduces stress and ensures they have time for what matters most.

3. **Engaging Storytelling**: The magical compass brings the concept of organization to life, making it relatable and fun for kids.

Tools to Support Learning for Chapter 5

To reinforce the concept of staying organized with calendars or planners, parents and teachers may find the following tools helpful:

- **My Weekly Planner Template**: Helps kids schedule their tasks and activities for the week, keeping track of their time.

- **Daily Task Organizer**: A simple, kid-friendly worksheet where children can list their tasks, assign time slots, and check them off when done.

- **Goal-Setting Calendar**: A colorful calendar template for kids to set daily or weekly goals and track their progress.

Part 2

Advanced Time Management Concepts

Take your time management skills to the next level! These chapters introduce powerful strategies to enhance productivity and focus.

Chapter 6

The Pareto Principle: The Secret of the 80/20 Rule

In This Chapter: Join Lily the Ladybug and her friends as they learn the secret of the 80/20 Rule—how focusing on a few key actions can lead to big results. Discover how this powerful principle can help you achieve more by working smarter, not harder.

Word to Remember: Focus

A Garden Insight

The friends were working in Lily's nearby garden, hoping to gather materials for decorating their treehouse. The garden, filled with vibrant flowers and buzzing bees, had a magical air that always put them at ease.

"Your garden looks amazing, Lily," Bella exclaimed, hopping through rows of blooming flowers. "How do you keep it looking so perfect?"

"Thanks, Bella!" Lily said, her wings fluttering with pride. "It wasn't always this way. Last summer, I spent hours trying to take care of every single plant, and I still couldn't keep up."

"So, what changed?" Timmy asked, tilting his head.

"That's when I learned about something called the **80/20 Rule**," Lily replied. "It means that a small part of your effort—just 20%—can bring most of the results, around 80%. I stopped trying to care for every plant equally and started focusing on the few that needed the most attention."

The Professor's Wisdom

As the friends leaned in to listen, Professor Timekeeper landed gracefully on a low branch.

"Lily is exactly right," he said with a hoot. "The **80/20 Rule**, also known as the **Pareto Principle**, is a powerful way to focus on what matters most. For example, in a garden, watering the thirstiest plants keeps the entire garden thriving."

What is the 80/20 Rule? The Professor Explains

The 80/20 Rule means that 20% of your actions bring 80% of your results. Focus on the few things that matter most to achieve the best results!

"Does that mean we don't need to do everything?" Max asked, scratching his head.

Professor Timekeeper nodded. "Trying to do everything at once is like trying to water an entire forest. Instead, focus your time and energy on the tasks that bring the biggest results. That's how you **work smarter, not harder**."

Applying the 80/20 Rule to the Treehouse

Timmy looked thoughtful. "So, for our treehouse, what would be the 20% that brings 80% of the results?"

Professor Timekeeper smiled. "That's a great question, Timmy. Start by asking: From the tasks you're focusing on right now, what's the one thing that will make the biggest difference? Is it building the ladder so you can reach the platform? Or painting the walls so it looks complete?"

The friends decided that attaching the ladder was the most important task. They worked together to complete it, and soon they could easily climb up and down the treehouse.

"This really works!" Max exclaimed. "Focusing on the ladder first made everything else easier!"

The 80/20 Rule in Life

As they rested, Max remembered something. "My uncle said that 20% of his customers make 80% of his sales. Is that the same thing?"

"Exactly, Max," said Professor Timekeeper. "In many areas of life and work, a small number of things often create the biggest impact. By focusing on those 20%, you can achieve great results without wasting effort."

Bella's ears perked up. "So, does that mean most problems (say 80%) come from just a few causes—like 20% of them?"

Professor Timekeeper nodded. "That's right, Bella. Often, a small number of issues cause most of the challenges. Identifying and addressing those key causes can solve many problems at once."

The 80/20 Rule in Action

Inspired by the discussion, the friends decided to try the 80/20 Rule in their own lives:

- Lily focused on watering her thirstiest plants first, then moved on to the others.

- Timmy cleaned the messiest part of his room first.

- Bella practiced the one trick that made the biggest difference in her performance.

- Max worked on the most important homework problems before tackling the rest.

By the end of the day, they had accomplished more than they expected and felt proud of themselves.

"Wow! The 80/20 Rule really works!" Max said, grinning.

Professor Timekeeper smiled. "Remember, my young adventurers: Always ask yourself, 'What's the 20% that will bring 80% of the results?' Focus on those first, and you'll be amazed at what you can achieve."

The friends cheered, excited to use the Pareto Principle in all their adventures.

For Parents and Teachers: Key Takeaways from Chapter 6

1. **Concept of the 80/20 Rule**: This chapter introduces children to the Pareto Principle, teaching them to focus on the few important tasks that bring the biggest results.

2. **Practical Application**: Through relatable examples, kids learn how to identify and prioritize the most impactful actions in their daily lives.

3. **Engaging Storytelling**: Lily's garden and the friends' examples bring the concept to life in a memorable and relatable way.

Tools to Support Learning for Chapter 6

To help children understand and apply the 80/20 Rule, parents and teachers may find these tools helpful:

- **20/80 Task Chart**: A worksheet where kids can list their tasks and identify the 20% that will bring 80% of the results.

- **Focus Tracker**: A tool for kids to record their most impactful actions each day and reflect on the results.

- **Big Impact Journal**: A simple notebook where kids can track which small actions made the biggest difference over time.

Chapter 7

Parkinson's Law:
The Power of Setting Deadlines

In This Chapter: Join Max the Monkey and his friends as they learn about the surprising power of deadlines. Discover how Parkinson's Law shows that tasks expand to fill the time available and how setting clear deadlines can help you get things done faster and more efficiently.

Word to Remember: **Deadlines**

The Art Challenge

The friends were gathered under their favorite shady tree in Clocksville, working on various tasks for the treehouse. Max the Monkey was busy with a drawing for an art contest but looked frustrated.

"I've been working on this drawing for hours, and it's still not done!" Max groaned. "I have until next week to finish it, but I don't know why it's taking so long."

Professor Timekeeper, perched nearby, observed thoughtfully. "Max, you're experiencing something called Parkinson's Law."

"What's Parkinson's Law?" Timmy the Tortoise asked, tilting his head.

What's Parkinson's Law? Professor Timekeeper Explains

Parkinson's Law states that tasks expand to fill the time available for their completion. For example, if you give yourself a week to finish your drawing, it might take the whole week. But if you set a shorter deadline, like two hours, you'll focus, work faster, and accomplish more.

Max's eyes widened. "You mean I could finish my drawing today if I set a shorter deadline?"

"Exactly!" said Professor Timekeeper. "Deadlines help you stay focused and use your time wisely. Without them, tasks can drag on much longer than they need to."

The Magic of Deadlines: A Treehouse Example

Lily the Ladybug added, "That's like when we said we'd decorate the treehouse 'someday.' Without a specific deadline, we kept putting it off. But when we decided to finish decorating the ladder before lunch, we got it done quickly!"

"That's a great example, Lily!" Professor Timekeeper said. "Deadlines don't just help you finish tasks—they also make you more focused and creative. Let's try an experiment. Max, set a timer for one hour and work on your drawing with all your focus. See what happens!"

Max grabbed his sketchpad and got to work, his tail swishing with determination. The friends cheered him on as he focused intensely on his art.

When the timer rang, Max proudly held up his completed drawing. "I did it! I can't believe I finished so quickly!"

Bella the Bunny clapped her paws. "That's amazing, Max! Deadlines really work!"

Professor Timekeeper smiled. "Remember, my young adventurers: When you set clear deadlines, you'll get more done in less time. Always challenge yourself to focus and finish efficiently."

The friends decided to use the power of deadlines in their own lives:

- **Max** planned to finish his homework before playtime instead of waiting until bedtime.

- **Bella** set a timer for her painting project to avoid distractions.

- **Lily** challenged herself to organize her tools before the sun set.

- **Timmy** decided to finish reading one book chapter before dinner.

The group decided to apply deadlines to their treehouse project, too. They set a goal to finish attaching the walls by the end of the afternoon. With this clear focus, they worked quickly and efficiently, and for the first time, they ended the day with a noticeable improvement to the treehouse.

"This is amazing!" Bella said. "Having deadlines keeps us moving forward!"

Max grinned. "Deadlines are like a magic spell for time management!"

Professor Timekeeper nodded. "And now you know the secret of Parkinson's Law. Use it wisely, and you'll achieve great things!"

For Parents and Teachers: Key Takeaways from Chapter 7

1. **Concept of Parkinson's Law**: This chapter introduces children to the idea that tasks take as long as the time you give them and that setting deadlines is a key strategy for time management.

2. **Practical Application**: Through relatable examples and a fun experiment, kids learn how deadlines can help them focus and work efficiently.

3. **Engaging Storytelling**: Max's drawing challenge and the friends' application of deadlines to the treehouse project bring the concept to life in an enjoyable and memorable way.

Tools to Support Learning for Chapter 7

To help children understand and apply the power of deadlines, parents and teachers may find these tools helpful:

- **Deadline Timer Chart**: A worksheet where kids can set timers for tasks and track how much they accomplish.

- **Task Breakdown Planner**: Helps kids divide larger tasks into smaller steps and assign deadlines to each step.

- **Achievement Tracker**: A simple journal where kids can record their deadlines and reflect on what they achieved by sticking to them.

Chapter 8

Eat Your Frog:
Doing the Hardest Task First

In This Chapter: Join Timmy the Tortoise and his friends as they learn the secret of tackling the hardest task first. Discover how the "Eat Your Frog" principle helps you overcome procrastination and achieve more by starting your day with your biggest challenge.

Word to Remember: Tackle

A Morning Challenge

The friends had gathered early at the treehouse project site, ready for another day of building. But while Bella, Max, and Lily were chatting excitedly about their plans, Timmy the Tortoise sat quietly, looking worried.

"What's wrong, Timmy?" Lily the Ladybug asked.

Timmy sighed. "I have this big school project to finish, but it feels so hard to start. Every time I think about it, I find something else to do instead—like organizing the nails for the treehouse!"

Professor Timekeeper, perched nearby, hooted warmly. "Timmy, you're not alone. Many people feel this way about their hardest tasks. But today, I'll teach you a secret that can help: the **'Eat Your Frog' principle**."

"Eat a frog?!" Max the Monkey exclaimed, making a funny face. "That sounds gross!"

Professor Timekeeper chuckled. "Don't worry, Max. It's not about eating a real frog! *'Eat Your Frog' is a way of saying that you should tackle your hardest or most important task first.* Once you've done it, everything else in your day feels easier."

Why Eat the Frog First?

Bella's ears twitched. "So, the frog is like the hardest task we need to do?"

"Exactly!" said Professor Timekeeper. "When you tackle your hardest task first, you feel accomplished and motivated to finish everything else. If you keep avoiding it, though, it stays in the back of your mind and makes you feel stuck."

"That's like yesterday," Lily said. "I kept putting off cleaning the toolshed because it seemed so boring. But when I finally did it first thing this morning, I felt so much better!"

"That's the magic of eating your frog," Professor Timekeeper said. "Timmy, why don't you try it? Start your day with your school project and see how it feels."

Eating the Frog in the Treehouse

Max tilted his head thoughtfully. "What about the treehouse, Professor? Is there a frog we need to eat here?"

"Great question, Max!" said Professor Timekeeper. "Think about the part of the treehouse that feels the hardest or most important—something you've been putting off."

"The safety railings!" Bella exclaimed. "We've been avoiding them because it's tricky to measure and attach."

Professor Timekeeper nodded. "Exactly! Let's start with the safety railings first today. If you finish them, the rest of the project will feel much easier."

Timmy's Victory

The next morning, Timmy came running to the treehouse site, looking proud and excited.

"I did it!" he announced. "I finished my school project first thing this morning. It wasn't as hard as I thought, and now I feel ready to take on the rest of the day!"

The friends cheered for Timmy.

"That's amazing, Timmy!" Bella said. "I'm going to try eating my frog too!"

Max grinned. "Me too! I'll start with my hardest homework problem tomorrow."

The friends turned their attention to the safety railings, determined to tackle them head-on. Working together, they measured, cut, and attached the pieces. By lunchtime, the railings were complete.

"This feels so good!" Max said. "The hardest part is done, and now the rest will be a breeze."

The Bigger Lesson

Professor Timekeeper spread his wings and addressed the group. "Remember, my young adventurers: The key to success is to eat your frog first. It may seem tough at first, but once it's done, you'll feel more accomplished and ready for anything."

Bella thought for a moment. "So, doing the hardest task first helps us reach our full potential?"

Professor Timekeeper smiled. "Exactly, Bella! Most people on Earth never realize their full potential. Even those who do often stop short of giving their best effort. They let distractions, fears, or delays hold them back, and many go through life without truly achieving what they're capable of. But I'm glad we're on this journey together because I know you'll be different. By learning to face challenges head-on, you're building the skills to unlock your true potential."

"We won't let our frogs stop us!" Max said confidently.

"That's the spirit, Max!" said Professor Timekeeper. "Now go out and show the world what you can do!"

For Parents and Teachers: Key Takeaways from Chapter 8

1. **Concept of 'Eat Your Frog'**: This chapter introduces children to the idea of tackling their hardest or most important task first to overcome procrastination and build momentum.

2. **Practical Application**: Through relatable examples, kids learn how starting with their toughest task can make the rest of their day more productive and enjoyable.

3. **Engaging Storytelling**: Timmy's struggle and success provide a memorable and motivating example of the power of tackling challenges head-on.

Tools to Support Learning for Chapter 8

To help children understand and apply the "Eat Your Frog" principle, parents and teachers may find these tools helpful:

- **Frog Task Tracker**: A worksheet where kids list their hardest tasks (frogs) and check them off as they complete them.

- **Morning Momentum Chart**: A simple tracker for kids to record the hardest task they tackled each morning and how they felt afterward.

- **Frog Rewards Jar**: A fun activity where kids earn small rewards (like stickers) each time they complete their frog task.

Work: 25 min
Break: 5 min
Repeat 4 times,
then take a longer break!"

Chapter 9

Pomodoro Technique:
Work, Rest, Repeat

In This Chapter: Join Timmy the Tortoise, Bella the Bunny, Max the Monkey, and Lily the Ladybug as they discover the magic of the Pomodoro Technique. Learn how working in short, focused bursts with regular breaks can help you stay energized and productive all day.

Word to Remember: Pomodoro (Work, Rest, Repeat)

A Distracted Start

At the treehouse site, the friends were trying to make progress, but Max the Monkey seemed especially restless.

"I have so much homework!" Max exclaimed, hopping up and down. "I try to focus, but I always get distracted before I finish anything!"

Bella nodded sympathetically. "I feel the same way, Max. It's hard to work on the treehouse for too long without feeling tired or bored."

Professor Timekeeper, who had been observing from his favorite perch, spread his wings. "My young builders, it sounds like you're trying to do too much at once. Let me teach you about a technique that can help: the **Pomodoro Technique.**"

What Is the Pomodoro Technique?

"*Pomodoro?*" Lily asked, tilting her head. "What does that mean?"

"It's named after the Italian word for tomato," Professor Timekeeper explained. "The creator of this method used a tomato-shaped timer! The idea is simple: work for a short, focused period—25 minutes—and then take a 5-minute break. After four work sessions, take a longer break, around 15 to 30 minutes.

The Pomodoro Technique helps you stay productive and energized by working in focused intervals, resting regularly, and breaking larger tasks into smaller, manageable pieces."

Timmy nodded thoughtfully. "So instead of working for hours and getting tired, we focus on one thing at a time and rest in between?"

"Exactly!" said Professor Timekeeper. "It keeps your mind fresh and helps you get more done without feeling overwhelmed. Why don't we try it right now with the treehouse project?"

The Friends Try the Pomodoro Technique

The friends decided to test the Pomodoro Technique by focusing on different parts of the treehouse:

- **Max** set a timer to work on measuring and cutting wood for 25 minutes.

- **Bella** focused on painting the treehouse walls.

- **Timmy** carefully sorted and prepared the tools.

- **Lily** organized the garden area near the treehouse.

When the timer rang, everyone took a 5-minute break to stretch, drink water, or chat.

"This feels so much better!" Max said, grinning. "I stayed focused the whole time because I knew a break was coming."

The friends completed four Pomodoro sessions that morning, pausing for a longer break to enjoy snacks and play tag in the park. By the afternoon, they had made more progress on the treehouse than ever before.

"This is amazing!" Bella said. "The breaks keep us from getting too tired, and we actually get more done."

Applying the Pomodoro Technique to Everyday Life

Professor Timekeeper smiled as he gathered the friends under the shady tree.

"That's the magic of the Pomodoro Technique," he said. "It teaches you to work smarter, not harder. By breaking your tasks into small, focused intervals and resting in between, you stay energized and productive."

Lily looked thoughtful. "So, we can use this for anything, not just the treehouse?"

"Absolutely," said Professor Timekeeper. "Homework, chores, hobbies—anything that feels overwhelming can be tackled with this technique. Focused effort, combined with regular breaks, is a powerful way to manage your time."

Max jumped up excitedly. "I'm going to use this for my homework tonight!"

"And I'll use it for organizing my garden tomorrow," Lily added.

Professor Timekeeper hooted warmly. "Remember, my adventurers: The key is balance. Work hard during your Pomodoro intervals, and enjoy your breaks to recharge. That's how you stay motivated and achieve great things."

The friends cheered, eager to use their new skill in all their adventures.

For Parents and Teachers: Key Takeaways from Chapter 9

1. **Concept of the Pomodoro Technique**: Introduces children to breaking tasks into short, focused intervals with regular breaks to maintain energy and focus.

2. **Practical Application**: Shows kids how to manage time effectively for homework, chores, or hobbies without feeling overwhelmed.

3. **Engaging Storytelling**: The friends' progress on the treehouse demonstrates how the technique works in a relatable and motivating way.

Tools to Support Learning for Chapter 9

To help children understand and apply the Pomodoro Technique, parents and teachers may find these tools helpful:

- **Pomodoro Timer Chart**: A visual tracker where kids can log their work and break sessions.

- **Focus Stopwatch**: Encourages kids to set timers for tasks and stay focused during work intervals.

- **Break Ideas List**: A list of fun and refreshing activities for kids to do during their 5-minute breaks.

Professor Timekeeper's three steps to deep work:

1. Choose one important task.
2. Find a quiet place to work.
3. Turn off distractions.

Chapter 10

Deep Work:
Focus Like a Champion

In This Chapter: Join Timmy the Tortoise, Bella the Bunny, Max the Monkey, and Lily the Ladybug as they discover the power of deep work—focusing completely on one important task without distractions. Learn how this skill helps you accomplish great things by giving your best effort to what matters most.

Word to Remember: Deep Work (Focus Like a Champion)

A Distracted Afternoon

At the treehouse site, the friends were hard at work—or at least trying to be.

Max the Monkey was supposed to be measuring wood, but he kept getting distracted by butterflies fluttering nearby. Bella the Bunny had started painting a sign for the treehouse but kept checking her phone every few minutes.

"This is so frustrating!" Max exclaimed, tossing his measuring tape aside. "I can't seem to focus!"

Bella nodded. "Me neither. Every time I try to concentrate, I get distracted!"

Professor Timekeeper, perched on a nearby branch, flapped his wings and hooted warmly. "Ah, my young builders, it sounds like you need to learn about the magic of deep work."

"Deep work?" Lily asked, tilting her head. "What's that, Professor?"

"It's the art of giving your full attention to one important task, without letting distractions get in the way," Professor Timekeeper explained. "It's like diving deep into a calm lake to find a hidden treasure. The deeper you go, the closer you get to achieving something great."

Learning the Secret of Deep Work

Timmy looked thoughtful. "How do we dive deep like that, Professor?"

Professor Timekeeper smiled. "The key is to follow three simple steps:

1. **Choose one important task.**

2. Find a quiet place to work.

3. Turn off distractions, like your phone or toys.

"When you focus fully on a task, your brain works better and faster. You'll be amazed at how much you can accomplish!"

"But what if I get bored?" Bella asked. "Sometimes it feels impossible to sit still."

"That's normal," Professor Timekeeper reassured her. "When you're new to deep work, your mind might wander. But with practice, it gets easier. Think of it like exercising a muscle—the more you practice, the stronger your focus will become."

Deep Work in Action

The friends decided to try deep work on tasks for the treehouse:

- **Max** chose to measure and cut wood, setting up a quiet area away from the fluttering butterflies.

- **Bella** turned off her phone and focused on painting the sign without interruptions.

- **Lily** organized the toolshed and avoided stopping to admire the flowers nearby.

- **Timmy** worked on sketching plans for the treehouse roof, sitting in a calm corner under the shady tree.

After an hour of focused effort, the friends regrouped to share their experiences.

"It was hard at first," Max admitted. "But once I got started, I didn't want to stop!"

"I finished my painting faster than I ever have before!" Bella said, her ears perking up. "I didn't even miss my phone."

Lily smiled. "I found all the tools we need for tomorrow's work. It felt so good to get it done!"

Professor Timekeeper clapped his wings. "Wonderful! Deep work is like a superpower. It helps you accomplish great things in less time. The more you practice, the easier it will become."

The Power of Deep Work

Max grinned. "So, deep work helps us focus like champions?"

"Exactly!" said Professor Timekeeper. "When you focus deeply, you unlock your best ideas and effort. Whether you're building a treehouse, doing homework, or working on a dream, deep work helps you succeed."

Timmy nodded. "I'm going to use this for my school projects, too!"

"And I'll focus on my garden chores tomorrow," Lily added.

Professor Timekeeper hooted proudly. "Remember, my adventurers: Deep work is your key to achieving great things. Dive deep, stay focused, and you'll reach new heights!"

The friends cheered, ready to use their newfound skill in all their tasks and adventures.

For Parents and Teachers: Key Takeaways from Chapter 10

1. **Concept of Deep Work**: This chapter teaches children the importance of distraction-free focus to accomplish significant tasks.

2. **Practical Application**: Simple steps and relatable examples show kids how to create a distraction-free environment and build focus as a skill.

3. **Engaging Storytelling**: The friends' challenges and successes demonstrate the benefits of deep work in a fun and relatable way.

Tools to Support Learning for Chapter 10

To help children understand and apply the concept of deep work, parents and teachers may find these tools helpful:

- **Deep Work Checklist**: A guide to help kids prepare for deep work sessions by choosing a task, finding a quiet spot, and turning off distractions.

- **Focus Timer**: A timer set for longer, focused sessions (e.g., 30–60 minutes) with breaks in between.

- **Reflection Journal**: A notebook for kids to record how they felt during deep work and what they accomplished.

Part 3

Applying Time Management

Now that you understand time management principles, it's time to apply them! These chapters focus on practical challenges, solutions, and activities to strengthen your time management habits.

KEY TIME MANAGEMENT BENEFITS:

* More free time for fun & growth
* Reduced stress
* Achieving goals
* Stronger friendships & teamwork

Chapter 11

The Benefits of Time Management: Reaping the Rewards

In This Chapter: Join Timmy, Bella, Max, Lily, and Professor Timekeeper as they reflect on their time management journey and discover how these skills have transformed their lives. Learn about the amazing benefits of time management, from achieving goals and reducing stress to finding more time for fun and growth.

Word to Remember: **Benefits** (Reaping the Rewards of Time Management)

Reflecting on the Journey

As the sun dipped below the horizon, the friends and Professor Timekeeper gathered around the glowing campfire near their almost-finished treehouse. The warm light danced on their happy faces, and the scent of pine filled the air.

"Look at how far we've come!" Max said, pointing at the treehouse, which now stood proudly with a sturdy ladder, walls, and even a painted sign.

"Last summer, we couldn't even finish the frame—we ran out of time," Bella said with a smile. "But now, we're so close to completing it!"

Professor Timekeeper nodded. "Indeed, my young adventurers. Your time management journey has been extraordinary. Tell me, what benefits have you noticed since learning these skills?"

Friends Share Their Time Management Stories

The friends took turns sharing their experiences:

- **Lily the Ladybug:** "I've had more time to care for my garden, and it looks more beautiful than ever! I'm even planting new flowers now because I'm not overwhelmed with unfinished tasks."

- **Timmy the Tortoise:** "I feel less stressed. Breaking big tasks into smaller steps has helped me focus, and I'm finally finishing my storybook project."

- **Bella the Bunny:** "Setting priorities has made such a difference! I'm painting more and even have time to practice new tricks."

- **Max the Monkey**: "Using the Pomodoro Technique helped me with my homework and left me with more free time to climb trees and play with you all!"

Professor Timekeeper listened with pride. "You see, time management isn't just about doing more—it's about living better. You've each gained something unique from your efforts, and together, you've achieved so much."

Uncovering the Benefits of Time Management

The friends reflected on the biggest benefits of time management as they admired their nearly finished treehouse:

1. More Free Time for Fun and Growth

"I never thought I'd have so much time for my hobbies!" Lily said. "And we still made progress on the treehouse!"

Professor Timekeeper added, "When you manage your time well, you create space for the things that make you happy and help you grow."

2. Reduced Stress

"I used to feel so rushed and worried," Timmy said. "Last summer, we couldn't even finish the frame. Now, we're almost done, and I feel calm, even with so much to do!"

"That's because a good plan clears your mind," Professor Timekeeper explained. "You don't have to carry all your tasks at once—you just focus on one step at a time."

3. Achieving Goals

Bella beamed. "It feels amazing to see the treehouse almost finished. Last year, we couldn't get past the frame, but this time, we've made incredible progress! We couldn't have done it without setting priorities and working together."

"And remember," Professor Timekeeper said, "the skills you've learned here will help you achieve even greater goals in the future."

4. Better Relationships

Max smiled. "We've all worked together so well. Learning to manage time has even made our teamwork stronger!"

Professor Timekeeper hooted softly. "That's the magic of shared time and effort. When you value your time, you value the time of others too."

Time Management: A Treasure for Life

As the campfire crackled, the friends gazed at their treehouse, feeling a deep sense of pride and accomplishment.

Professor Timekeeper spread his wings. "Remember, my adventurers, time is one of your most valuable treasures. When you manage it wisely, you create a life filled with joy, success, and connection."

The friends cheered, raising their hands together. "To time management and all its rewards!"

They knew that these skills weren't just for building a treehouse—they were tools they would carry with them for the rest of their lives. Whether in school, at home, or on future adventures, they were ready to face challenges, seize opportunities, and make the most of every moment.

For Parents and Teachers: Key Takeaways from Chapter 11

1. **The Rewards of Time Management**: This chapter highlights how effective time management leads to several benefits including reduced stress, more free time, better relationships, and achieving goals.

2. **Practical Inspiration**: By sharing the friends' personal stories, children can see how these lessons apply to their own lives and recognize the rewards of practicing time management.

3. **Encouragement to Reflect**: The chapter encourages children to reflect on their own progress and celebrate the positive changes they've experienced through better time management.

Tools to Support Learning for Chapter 11

To help children understand and appreciate the rewards of time management, parents and teachers may find these tools helpful:

*   **Reward Reflection Chart**: A worksheet for kids to list what they gained from managing their time better, like new hobbies or finished tasks.

*   **Goal Achievement Tracker**: A chart where kids can record goals they've achieved and how time management helped them succeed.

*   **Thank You Notes for Time**: A fun activity where kids write a short letter thanking themselves for using their time wisely, reinforcing the value of their efforts.

Chapter 12

Time Management Challenges and Solutions

In This Chapter: Join Timmy, Bella, Max, Lily, and Professor Timekeeper as they explore common challenges to managing time effectively and discover practical solutions to overcome them. Learn how to tackle procrastination, distractions, and unexpected interruptions like a true time management master.

Word to Remember: Solutions

The Treehouse Adventure: Progress Amid Challenges

The friends were hard at work on their treehouse, and this time, things were moving along better than before. Max the Monkey had finished hammering the frame, Bella the Bunny had painted one wall a bright and cheerful color, and Lily the Ladybug was organizing the tools neatly in the corner, among many things they had already accomplished—far more than during their previous attempt to build the treehouse.

"This is looking amazing!" Timmy the Tortoise said with a smile. "We've made so much progress since last summer."

But just as they started feeling proud, some challenges began to creep in. Max got distracted by a flock of colorful birds nearby. Bella couldn't resist bouncing her ball across the yard, and Lily felt overwhelmed by her long to-do list, unsure where to start.

Professor Timekeeper fluttered down from his perch on a nearby tree branch, smiling kindly. "Well done so far, my young adventurers! You've come a long way. But remember, every great journey comes with its own set of challenges. The key is learning how to handle them."

Identifying Challenges

The friends gathered under the tree to discuss their struggles.

1. Procrastination:
"Sometimes I know what I need to do, but I just keep putting it off," Max admitted, scratching his head.

"That's called procrastination," Professor Timekeeper explained. "It happens when a task feels too hard or boring, so we delay it."

2. Distractions:

Bella chimed in. "I keep getting distracted by everything around me. It's hard to focus!"

Professor Timekeeper nodded. "Distractions are a big challenge, but there are effective ways to handle them. With the right strategies and tools, you can train your mind to stay focused and accomplish your tasks."

3. Feeling Overwhelmed:

"I feel like there's just too much to do," Lily said, looking at her long list. "It's hard to know where to start!"

"That's overwhelm," the Professor said gently. "It can freeze you in place, but breaking tasks into smaller steps can help."

4. Interruptions:

"And what about when someone calls me away while I'm in the middle of something?" Timmy asked.

"Interruptions are part of life," Professor Timekeeper said. "But learning to handle them wisely makes all the difference."

Finding Solutions

Professor Timekeeper offered strategies for each challenge.

1. Procrastination Solution: The Two-Minute Rule

"If you're procrastinating, start small," Professor Timekeeper said. "Commit to working on the task for just two minutes. Once you start, you'll often feel like continuing."

Max decided to try it by hammering just one nail into the treehouse frame. "Hey, this isn't so bad! I can keep going!"

2. Distractions Solution: The Focus Zone

"Create a Focus Zone," the Professor suggested. "Find a quiet spot, turn off distractions like your phone, and set a timer to stay focused for a short period."

Bella turned off her phone and worked on painting the treehouse walls. "Wow, I didn't even notice the time passing!" she said.

3. Feeling Overwhelmed Solution: Start Small

"If you feel overwhelmed, choose one small task to start with," Professor Timekeeper said. "Once you complete it, you'll feel more confident to tackle the rest."

Lily decided to organize one toolbox at a time instead of worrying about the whole garden. "It's amazing how small steps make a big difference!"

4. Interruptions Solution: Pause, Plan, and Communicate

"When interruptions happen, pause and plan," Professor Timekeeper advised. "If you're in the middle of a task, make a note of where you stopped so you can return to it later. And if it's something that can wait—like a friend calling while you're doing homework—politely let them know you'll call back when you're done."

Timmy got called away to help a neighbor, so he quickly noted where he stopped on his list and returned to finish his task afterward. Later, Max shared, "While I was working on my math homework, Bella called to invite me to play. I told her I'd join her after I finished. It felt great to stay focused!"

Professor Timekeeper hooted in approval. "That's an excellent example, Max! Learning to communicate your priorities is an important part of managing interruptions."

A Lesson in Resilience

By the end of the day, the friends had overcome their challenges and made impressive progress on the treehouse.

"This is incredible!" Max said, admiring their work. "I thought we were stuck, but now we're closer than ever to finishing!"

Professor Timekeeper beamed. "Remember, my young adventurers, challenges are part of every journey. But with the right solutions, you can overcome them and keep moving forward."

The friends cheered, excited to use their new strategies in all their future adventures.

For Parents and Teachers: Key Takeaways from Chapter 12

1. **Common Challenges:** This chapter identifies common time management challenges like procrastination, distractions, feeling overwhelmed, and interruptions.

2. **Practical Solutions:** Children learn simple, actionable strategies to address these challenges and build resilience.

3. **Relatable Storytelling:** The friends' struggles and successes make the concepts engaging and memorable.

Tools to Support Learning for Chapter 12

To help children apply these solutions, parents and teachers may find the following tools helpful:

- **Focus Zone Checklist:** A guide for kids to set up a distraction-free workspace.

- **Two-Minute Starter Chart:** A worksheet where kids list tasks they can start in two minutes.

- **Overwhelm Buster Worksheet:** A tool to break big tasks into smaller, manageable steps.

- **Pause-and-Plan Journal:** A space for kids to jot down where they stopped and how to restart after an interruption.

By learning to tackle challenges with these strategies, children will develop confidence and adaptability, key ingredients for time management mastery!

Chapter 13

Time Management Activities and Practice

In This Chapter: Put your time management skills to the test with Timmy, Bella, Max, Lily, and Professor Timekeeper. Learn how to set SMART goals, track your progress, and combine advanced techniques like prioritization, routines, and deep work to accomplish big tasks—just like finishing the treehouse!

Word to Remember: Practice

Time Management in Practice: Achieving SMART Goals Together

The friends gathered under their now nearly-complete treehouse, proud of their progress but eager to finish the final touches.

"We've come so far!" Bella said, looking at the painted walls and sturdy ladder. "But there's still so much to do—how can we make sure we finish everything before the vacation ends?"

Professor Timekeeper landed on a low branch, smiling warmly. "This is the perfect opportunity to use everything you've learned. Let's also add one more powerful tool to your time management treasure chest: **SMART goals.**"

SMART Goals: Your Key to Effective Goal-Setting

"What are SMART goals?" Lily asked, her notebook ready.

Professor Timekeeper explained, "SMART stands for:
- **Specific:** Know exactly what you want to accomplish.

- **Measurable:** Make sure you can track your progress.

- **Achievable:** Set goals that are realistic.

- **Relevant:** Focus on what's important.

- **Time-bound:** Give yourself a deadline to complete it.

"Let's create a SMART goal for finishing the treehouse!"

Setting a SMART Goal

Together, the friends came up with this goal:

Goal: Complete the treehouse (Specific) by adding the decorations, hanging the swing, and building the roof (Measurable) within two days (Time-bound). It's achievable because they planned time to work together, and it's relevant because finishing the treehouse is their priority.

"Now that's a SMART goal!" Max said excitedly.

Professor Timekeeper nodded. "With a clear goal in mind, let's use the tools you've learned to make it happen."

Activity 1: Prioritizing and Routines

The friends divided their tasks:

- **Max** focused on hanging the swing.

- **Bella** worked on painting decorations.

- **Lily** organized the supplies for the roof.

- **Timmy** built the roof, piece by piece.

"We'll follow our routine: start with the hardest tasks and work in focused sessions," Lily reminded them.

Activity 2: Using Advanced Techniques

As they worked, the friends used advanced techniques to stay on track:

1. **Pomodoro Technique:** Each friend worked for 25 minutes, then took a 5-minute break. During their breaks, they stretched, shared snacks, and cheered each other on.

2. **Deep Work:** Timmy and Lily practiced deep work, staying focused while building the roof and organizing the materials.

3. **Big Rock Prioritization:** They tackled the hardest tasks—the roof and swing—before moving on to decorations.

Tracking Progress and Overcoming Challenges

"Let's track our progress!" Bella said, marking tasks off their planner.

They also used a **Goal-Setting Worksheet** that Professor Timekeeper had given them. Each friend wrote down their mini-goals for the day and checked them off as they completed them.

When Max struggled to hang the swing, he paused to ask for help. Timmy joined him, and together they finished the task.

"Asking for help is also part of good time management," Professor Timekeeper reminded them.

The Rewards of Time Management Practice: Achieving Success Together

By the end of the day, the treehouse was complete—decorations, swing, roof, and all! The friends stood back, admiring their hard work.

"This feels amazing," Bella said, looking at their finished masterpiece. "We couldn't have done it without practicing everything we learned."

Professor Timekeeper nodded proudly. "You've shown that with SMART goals, planning, and teamwork, even the biggest challenges can be conquered. Keep practicing these skills, and they'll serve you well for a lifetime."

The friends cheered, ready to celebrate their success in the finished treehouse!

For Parents and Teachers: Key Takeaways from Chapter 13

1. **Practical Application:** This chapter emphasizes applying all previously learned time management skills—prioritization, routines, breaking tasks, focus techniques, and goal setting—to real-life challenges.

2. **SMART Goals:** Introduces children to SMART goal-setting and helps them see how clear, actionable goals lead to success.

3. **Teamwork and Resilience:** Shows how collaboration and adaptability help overcome challenges and achieve shared goals.

Tools to Support Learning for Chapter 13

To help children practice and refine their time management skills, parents and teachers may find these tools helpful:

- **SMART Goal Worksheet:** A template for kids to set and track Specific, Measurable, Achievable, Relevant, and Time-bound goals.

- **Project Tracker:** A chart for breaking down tasks into smaller steps and tracking progress.

- **Reflection Journal:** Encourages kids to reflect on what worked, what didn't, and how they felt after completing their tasks.

MASTER TIME MANAGEMENT LESSONS
☒ Prioritization & Routines
☒ Breaking Tasks into Steps
☒ Using Planners & Calendars
☒ Smart Techniques (Pomodoro,
   80/20 Rule, Deep Work)
☒ Tackling Challenges & Distractions
☒ SMART Goal Setting

Time
Management
Lessons

Time Management Maste

TIME
MANAGEMENT

Chapter 14

Time Management Masters: A Review of Lessons, Takeaways, and Master Time Management Summary Chart

In This Chapter: Reflect on the incredible journey with Timmy, Bella, Max, Lily, and Professor Timekeeper as they review the key lessons learned. Celebrate how mastering time management principles has transformed their lives—and yours too!

Word to Remember: Time Management Mastery

A Moment of Reflection

The sun was setting over the lively town of Clocksville as the friends gathered one last time in their nearly finished treehouse. The beams were steady, the ladder sturdy, and the walls painted with vibrant colors. For the first time, they could look around and see the result of their hard work, determination, and, most importantly, their new time management skills.

"Can you believe it?" Bella said, her eyes sparkling. "Last year, we couldn't even finish the frame. Now, look at this!"

Professor Timekeeper hooted proudly. "You've come a long way, my young adventurers. You've not only built a magnificent treehouse but also mastered skills that will help you throughout your lives."

The friends nodded in agreement, each reflecting on the lessons they had learned.

Reviewing Key Lessons

The group decided to revisit the time management principles they had discovered along their journey.

1. Prioritization: The Treasure Map of Time

"Remember how we learned to focus on what matters most?" Lily said. "Prioritizing tasks made such a difference."

Professor Timekeeper smiled. "Indeed! Always ask yourself: What is the most important thing to do right now?"

2. Routines: The Magic of Daily Rituals

Timmy added, "Creating routines helped me stay consistent. Doing little things every day really adds up!"

"Routines are the backbone of time management," the Professor agreed. "They make big goals achievable, one small step at a time."

3. Breaking Tasks into Smaller Steps

"Task Mountain!" Max shouted. "I'll never forget how breaking things into steps made even the biggest challenges manageable."

"Big tasks become small victories," said the Professor. "And small victories lead to great success."

4. Using Tools: Calendars and Planners

"Using the calendar was so helpful," Bella said. "I stopped forgetting things and felt more organized."

"Tools like calendars are your compass," the Professor explained. "They keep you on track and focused."

5. Advanced Techniques: Working Smarter, Not Harder

"Taking breaks with the **Pomodoro Technique** kept me from feeling tired," Max shared. "I worked in short bursts and felt so refreshed after each break!"

"And the **80/20 Rule** taught me to focus on the few things that bring big results," Lily added. "It's amazing how much you can accomplish by focusing on what truly matters."

"Each of these techniques helps you work smarter, not harder," Professor Timekeeper noted.

6. Tackling Challenges with Advanced Tools

Timmy nodded, "The **Eat Your Frog** strategy made starting my day so much easier. Tackling the hardest task first really gives me momentum."

"The **Parkinson's Law** principle was a game changer for me," Bella chimed in. "Setting clear deadlines helped me finish faster and stay focused."

"And let's not forget about **Deep Work**," Lily said thoughtfully. "When I really focused on one task without distractions, I got so much more done."

Professor Timekeeper nodded proudly. "You've truly embraced these strategies, and that's the hallmark of a time management master. By combining focus, prioritization, and commitment with the time management principles, tools, and strategies you've mastered, you've not only overcome challenges but also unlocked your full potential. Remember, these resources are like a treasure chest—always available to help you tackle new adventures and achieve even greater success in life."

7. Overcoming Challenges

Timmy smiled. "Interruptions used to ruin my focus, but now I know how to handle them."

"The key is adaptability," said Professor Timekeeper. "Pause, plan, and keep going."

SMART Goals and Looking Ahead

Professor Timekeeper brought out a scroll. "Before we celebrate, let's set some SMART goals for the future. Remember, goals should be:

- **Specific**: What do you want to achieve?
- **Measurable**: How will you track your progress?
- **Achievable**: Is it realistic?
- **Relevant**: Why does it matter to you?
- **Time-bound**: When will you complete it?"

Each friend set a goal:

- Bella aimed to paint a mural in the town square by the end of summer.
- Max planned to read three books in the next month.

- Lily decided to expand her garden with new flowers by the next season.
- Timmy wanted to write a short story about their adventures before school started.

The friends wrote down their goals, feeling confident and inspired.

A Celebration of Growth

As the moon rose, the friends hung a sign on the treehouse: **"Time Management Masters."** They shared a feast and reflected on how far they had come.

Professor Timekeeper raised a wing. "Remember, mastering time management isn't about perfection. It's about progress. Keep applying what you've learned, and you'll continue to achieve amazing things."

The friends cheered, ready to take their skills into every new adventure ahead.

For Parents and Teachers: Key Takeaways from Chapter 14

1. **Comprehensive Review**: This chapter revisits every major time management principle covered in the book, reinforcing key lessons.

2. **Celebrate Progress**: Children see the value of reflection and celebrating achievements as part of personal growth.

3. **Goal-Setting for the Future**: Introducing SMART goals ensures that kids can set actionable, realistic objectives for continued success.

Tools to Support Learning for Chapter 14

- **Achievement Reflection Worksheet**: A guide for kids to list their accomplishments and reflect on how time management helped them succeed.

- **SMART Goal-Setting Template**: A structured worksheet to help children create and track meaningful goals.

- **Mastery Badge Printable**: A fun badge kids can print and wear to celebrate becoming Time Management Masters.

Closing Words

The journey of time management is never truly over. With every goal you set, every step you take, and every lesson you learn, you grow closer to mastering your time and your life. Now, it's your turn to take these skills and make your dreams a reality—just like Timmy, Bella, Max, and Lily!

Your Time Management Guide

As you embark on your own time management adventure, here's a handy guide to review all the key lessons, tools, and techniques we've explored. Think of this chart as your very own treasure map, guiding you to success and balance in every part of your day.

Master Time Management: Summary Chart

Concept/Technique	Key Insight	Practical Tip
Prioritization	Focus on tasks that matter most.	Use the **Blank Prioritization Table** to rank tasks by importance.
Routines	Establish daily habits to build consistency.	Create a personalized **My Weekly Planner Template**.
Task Breakdown	Divide big tasks into smaller, manageable steps.	Use the **Task Breakdown Worksheet** for clarity and direction.
Using a Calendar	Plan and organize tasks to stay on track.	Apply the **Time Management Compass** to map out your days.

Concept/Technique	Key Insight	Practical Tip
80/20 Rule	Focus on the 20% of efforts that yield 80% of results.	Use the **20/80 Task Chart** to identify high-impact actions.
Parkinson's Law	Set tight deadlines to prevent tasks from expanding.	Try the **Deadline Timer Chart** to finish tasks quickly.
Pomodoro Technique	Work in focused bursts with breaks.	Follow the **Pomodoro Timer Chart** for structured work sessions.
Deep Work	Focus deeply on one task for maximum productivity.	Prepare using the **Deep Work Checklist** and record progress in the **Focus Tracker**.
SMART Goals	Set Specific, Measurable, Achievable, Relevant, Time-bound goals.	Use the **SMART Goals Worksheet** to define and track progress.
Time Audit	Understand where your time goes to identify improvements.	Use the **My 24-Hour Time Tracking Chart**.
Interruptions Management	Handle distractions and stay on task.	Keep a **Distraction Log** and practice the "Pause and Plan" technique.
Motivation and Rewards	Celebrate small wins to stay motivated.	Create a **Frog Rewards Jar** to recognize achievements.
Review and Adjust	Regularly evaluate and adapt your strategies.	Use the **Reflection Journal** to assess what works and what doesn't.

Part 4

Time Management Assessment and Tools

This section provides self-assessment tools and practical resources to help you track progress and improve your time management skills.

Time Management Self-Assessment
HOW HAVE YOU GROWN?
☒ Prioritization & Routines ✓
☒ Breaking Tasks into Steps ✓
☒ Using Planners & Calendars ✓
☒ Smart Techniques (Pomodoro, 80/20 Rule, Deep Work) ✓
☒ Tackling Challenges &
☒ SMART Goal Setting

Chapter 15

Time Management Self-Assessment Quiz for Children

In This Chapter: Discover how well you've mastered time management by taking this fun and insightful self-assessment quiz. Reflect on your daily habits, celebrate your progress, and uncover opportunities to grow as you continue your journey to becoming a Time Management Master!

Self-assessment is more than just a tool—it's a way to celebrate what you've achieved, learn from your challenges, and take actionable steps toward mastering time management.

Word to Remember: **Self-Reflection**

Welcome to the Self-Assessment Quiz!

Are you ready to see how well you're managing your time? Answer the following questions honestly and reflect on your daily habits. Use the scale below:

- **1 = Never**
- **2 = Sometimes**
- **3 = Often**
- **4 = Always**

The Quiz:

1. I set clear priorities for my tasks and activities.

2. I have a daily routine that helps me stay organized.

3. I break large tasks into smaller, manageable steps.

4. I use a calendar or planner to track my tasks and events.

5. I stay focused on one task at a time without distractions.

6. I use tools like the Pomodoro Timer or Goal-Setting Worksheets to manage my time effectively.

7. I adapt my schedule when unexpected things happen.

8. I ask for help when I need it.

9. I review my progress at the end of the day or week.

10. I feel in control of my time and can balance work, play, and rest.

For Parents and Teachers

This self-assessment quiz is designed to help children reflect on their time management skills. Encourage them to answer honestly and use the results as a starting point for improvement.

Tools to Support This Chapter

- **Reflection Journal:** Encourage kids to track their progress over time.

- **Progress Tracker:** A chart to log quiz scores and set goals for improvement.

Chapter 16

❧※❧

Time Management
Self-Assessment Quiz Results and
Comprehensive Summary Chart:
Your Time Management Toolkit

In This Chapter: Learn how to interpret your quiz results, celebrate your time management strengths, and discover strategies to improve in areas where you need support.

Word to Remember: Insights for Growth

Understanding Your Score

Now that you've taken the quiz, add up your total points and see how you score:

- **30–40 points: Time Management Champion**
  Congratulations! You're on your way to becoming a Time Management Master. Keep using the tools and techniques you've learned to stay organized and achieve your goals.

- **20–29 points: Time Management Apprentice**
  Great work! You have good skills but can refine a few areas. Focus on improving your routines and using tools like planners and trackers.

- **10–19 points: Time Management Explorer**
  You're starting your journey. Focus on setting priorities and breaking big tasks into smaller steps. Use the tools in this book to help you stay on track.

- **0–9 points: Time Management Beginner**
  It's okay to start small! Begin with one skill, like creating a simple daily routine, and build from there. Progress happens one step at a time!

Personalized Tips for Improvement

Based on your score, here are targeted strategies to help you grow:

1. **For Setting Priorities:** Use the Big Rock Exercise to focus on what matters most.

2. **For Daily Routines:** Create a schedule using the Weekly Planner Template.

3. **For Breaking Tasks:** Try the Task Breakdown Worksheet to make big goals manageable.

4. **For Staying Focused:** Practice the Pomodoro Technique to improve concentration.

5. **For Tracking Progress:** Use the Goal-Setting Exercise Worksheet to review your achievements.

Tools to Support This Chapter

- **Comprehensive Summary Chart:** A guide to the tools and concepts that can help improve each area.
- **Goal-Setting Calendar:** Helps children set and track weekly goals based on their quiz results.

Closing Words

This quiz is just the beginning of your journey to mastering time management. Whether you're already a champion or just starting, remember that every small improvement brings you closer to achieving your goals. Keep practicing and enjoy the rewards of managing your time effectively!

Your Guide to Mastering Time Management

As you continue your journey to mastering time management, here's a comprehensive summary of all the tools and concepts we've explored in this book. Use this chart as your roadmap to success!

Comprehensive Summary Chart: Your Time Management Toolkit

Note: *Chapters 17 to 32 are dedicated to the tools themselves. These chapters provide detailed instructions, examples, and blank templates to help you apply the time management principles and strategies discussed in earlier chapters.*

Chapter	Key Concept	Associated Tool
Chapter 2	Treasure Map of Time: Prioritize	Blank Prioritization Table *(Chapter 21)*: Categorize tasks into Red, Yellow, and Blue.
Chapter 3	Daily Rituals: Build Consistency	Weekly Routine Planner *(Chapter 22)*: Blend responsibilities and fun.

Chapter	Key Concept	Associated Tool
Chapter 4	Task Mountain: Break into Steps	*Task Breakdown Worksheet (Chapter 23): Divide tasks into smaller steps.*
Chapter 5	Time Compass: Organize with a Calendar	Calendar or Planner Template *(Chapter 24)*: Assign time slots and track tasks.
Chapter 6	80/20 Rule: Focus on Impactful Actions	20/80 Task Chart *(Chapter 27)*: Identify tasks yielding the biggest results.
Chapter 7	Deadlines: Work Efficiently	Deadline Timer Tracker *(Chapter 28)*: Set time limits and log achievements.
Chapter 8	Hardest Task First: Tackle Challenges	Frog Task Tracker *(Chapter 29)*: Prioritize and complete the hardest tasks.
Chapter 9	Work and Rest: Stay Energized	Pomodoro Timer Chart *(Chapter 25)*: Log intervals for focus and breaks.
Chapter 10	Distraction-Free Focus: Productivity Boost	Deep Work Checklist *(Chapter 26)*: Steps for focused work sessions.
Chapter 11	Rewards: More Free Time and Less Stress	Time Management Reflection Journal *(Chapter 30):* Reflect on achievements and stress reduction.
Chapter 12	Overcoming Interruptions and Procrastination	Pause-and-Plan Journal: Resume tasks efficiently after interruptions.
Chapter 13	Strengthen Time Management Skills	SMART Goals Worksheet: Track Specific, Measurable, Achievable, Relevant, Time-bound goals.
Chapter 15	Self-Assessment Quiz	Self-Assessment Quiz Worksheet *(Chapter 31):* Reflect on time management strengths and areas of improvement.

Chapter	Key Concept	Associated Tool
Chapter 16	Results and Improvement	Self-Assessment Results Tracker *(Chapter 32)*: Create a personalized improvement plan.
Chapter 17 (Toolkit)	Awareness: Track Daily Activities	24-Hour Time Tracking Chart: Reflect and improve time use.
Chapter 18 (Toolkit)	Distraction Awareness and Solutions	Distraction Log: Identify and mitigate distractions.
Chapter 19 (Toolkit)	Setting Realistic and Actionable Goals	Goal-Setting Exercise Worksheet: Define and achieve meaningful goals.
Chapter 20 (Toolkit)	Focus on High-Impact Tasks	Big Rock Exercise: Identify and prioritize critical tasks.
Chapter 21 (Toolkit)	Categorizing Priorities	Blank Prioritization Table: Refine prioritization by categorizing tasks.
Chapter 22 (Toolkit)	Weekly Routine Building	Weekly Routine Planner: Plan and structure weekly routines effectively.
Chapter 23 (Toolkit)	Breaking Down Complex Tasks	Task Breakdown Worksheet: Organize complex tasks into manageable pieces.
Chapter 24 (Toolkit)	Time Blocking	Calendar or Planner Template: Time-block tasks to enhance productivity.
Chapter 25 (Toolkit)	Pomodoro Implementation	Pomodoro Timer Chart: Visualize focused work and break intervals.
Chapter 26 (Toolkit)	Preparing for Deep Focus	Deep Work Checklist: Establish steps for distraction-free focus sessions.
Chapter 27 (Toolkit)	Pareto Prioritization	20/80 Task Chart: Pinpoint and prioritize the most impactful tasks.
Chapter 28 (Toolkit)	Deadline Awareness	Deadline Timer Tracker: Build efficiency with clear deadlines.

Chapter	Key Concept	Associated Tool
Chapter 29 (Toolkit)	Tackling Difficult Tasks	Frog Task Tracker: Address the hardest tasks first for momentum.
Chapter 30 (Toolkit)	Reflection on Time Management Progress	Time Management Reflection Journal: Reflect on progress and areas to improve.
Chapter 31 (Toolkit)	Enhancing Assessment Insights	Self-Assessment Quiz Worksheet: Support improved reflection through detailed quizzes.
Chapter 32 (Toolkit)	Planning for Growth	Self-Assessment Results and Improvement Tracker: Design an actionable improvement strategy.

For Parents and Teachers: Key Takeaways from Chapter 16

The **Time Management Self-Assessment Quiz** helps children recognize their strengths and pinpoint areas for growth. By reviewing their scores together, you can foster self-reflection and **guide them in setting realistic, achievable goals**.

As we transition into the **practical tools section (Chapters 17–32)**, your support will be essential in helping children apply the concepts they've learned. These upcoming chapters provide **step-by-step instructions, real-life examples, and blank templates** to help children develop effective time management habits.

Encourage your child to **engage actively with each tool**, reflect on their progress, and **experiment with different strategies** to discover what works best for them. Your guidance in discussing these tools, reinforcing their importance, and **celebrating small successes** will help build confidence and make time management a lifelong skill.

Chapter 17

My 24-Hour Time Tracking Chart

In This Chapter: You will find a chart to help children track their time for a day. This chart provides an example of how you can track and manage your time throughout the day. It helps you visualize how you spend your time and identify areas where you can improve your time management.

Word to Remember: Time Tracking

Just like Timmy, Bella, Max, and Lily used their time tracking chart to balance work on their treehouse with fun activities, you can use this tool to see how your day is structured. Remember, everyone's schedule is different, so feel free to adjust this chart according to your personal needs and activities. Use it as a starting point to create your own time tracking chart and take control of your day.

Time	Activity	Duration
6:00 - 7:00	Wake up & morning routine	1 hour
7:00 - 7:30	Breakfast	30 minutes
7:30 - 8:00	Get ready for school	30 minutes
8:00 - 3:00	School	7 hours
3:00 - 3:30	Afternoon snack	30 minutes
3:30 - 5:00	Homework	1.5 hours
5:00 - 6:00	Extracurricular activity	1 hour
6:00 - 7:00	Free time	1 hour
7:00 - 7:30	Dinner	30 minutes
7:30 - 8:00	Evening routine	30 minutes
8:00 - 9:00	Relaxing/Reading	1 hour
9:00 - 9:30	Getting ready for bed	30 minutes
9:30 - 6:00	Sleep	8.5 hours

In addition to the Specimen Chart provided earlier, here is a blank table that you can use to prioritize your activities based on their value and urgency. This table is a helpful tool for planning and organizing your tasks throughout the day, allowing you to identify opportunities to save time and stay focused on your priorities. Feel free to customize this table according to your own needs and preferences. Use it to become more productive and achieve your goals efficiently.

From	To	Activity	Value to You?	Did it have to be done?	Did it have to be done now?	Did it have to be done quite so well?	Ideas to Save Time
6:00 AM	7:00 AM						
7:00 AM	8:00 AM						
8:00 AM	9:00 AM						
9:00 AM	10:00 AM						
10:00 AM	11:00 AM						
11:00 AM	12:00 PM						
12:00 PM	1:00 PM						
1:00 PM	2:00 PM						
2:00 PM	3:00 PM						

From	To	Activity	Value to You?	Did it have to be done?	Did it have to be done now?	Did it have to be done quite so well?	Ideas to Save Time
3:00 PM	4:00 PM						
4:00 PM	5:00 PM						
5:00 PM	6:00 PM						
6:00 PM	7:00 PM						
7:00 PM	8:00 PM						
8:00 PM	9:00 PM						
9:00 PM	10:00 PM						
10:00 PM	11:00 PM						
11:00 PM	12:00 AM						
12:00 AM	1:00 AM						
1:00 AM	2:00 AM						
2:00 AM	3:00 AM						

From	To	Activity	Value to You?	Did it have to be done?	Did it have to be done now?	Did it have to be done quite so well?	Ideas to Save Time
3:00 AM	4:00 AM						
4:00 AM	5:00 AM						
5:00 AM	6:00 AM						

For Parents and Teachers: Key Takeaways from Chapter 17

The 24-Hour Time Tracking Chart is a valuable tool to help children visualize how they spend their time and make adjustments for better productivity and balance. By tracking their daily activities, they can identify where their time goes, recognize patterns, and find opportunities to improve their time management skills.

Encourage your child to use this chart thoughtfully, discussing what activities add the most value to their day. Help them reflect on questions like:

- Are they spending enough time on important tasks like studying, sleep, and self-care?

- Are there time wasters that could be reduced?

- How can they better balance school, hobbies, and relaxation?

As you guide them through this process, remind them that everyone's schedule is different, and time tracking is not about perfection but about building awareness and making small, meaningful improvements. Celebrate their progress, and help them develop a daily routine that works best for them!

Chapter 18

Distraction Log for Children

In This Chapter: You'll discover a powerful time management tool—the Distraction Log—designed to help children identify their biggest distractions and develop smart strategies to stay focused and on track.

Are distractions like TV, phones, or social media keeping you from staying focused and achieving your goals? Don't worry—you're not alone!

Word to Remember: Distraction Log

The **Distraction Log for Children** is designed to help you recognize distractions, analyze their impact, and find effective ways to maintain focus. This tool consists of two sections:

- A **filled sample log** to guide you.
- A **blank log** for you to fill out on your own.

Why Use a Distraction Log?

The goal of this log is to help you track distractions throughout the day, understand their impact, and brainstorm ways to manage or eliminate them. With practice, you'll find it easier to stay focused and achieve your goals.

How to Use the Distraction Log:

1. **Print the Template:** Start with a blank log to make tracking easy.

2. **Record Distractions:** Throughout the day, write down:
   - The time the distraction occurred.
   - What the distraction was.
   - How long it lasted.

3. **Review Your Log:** At the end of the day, sit down with a parent, guardian, or mentor to discuss the distractions.

4. **Brainstorm Solutions:** For each distraction, come up with strategies to overcome it in the future.

5. **Keep It Handy:** Refer to the log whenever distractions creep in, using it as a reminder of your progress and strategies.

Filled Distraction Log Example

Here's an example of a completed log to guide you. It includes the time, type of distraction, duration, and actionable strategies to overcome them. Use it as a reference for creating your own.

Time of Day	Distraction	Duration	How it Made Me Feel	Strategy to Overcome
9:00 AM	TV	30 minutes	Distracted	Turn off the TV and set a timer to watch it later.
10:15 AM	Friend calling	10 minutes	Distracted and Excited	Politely let your friend know it's study time and promise to call back after completing your work.
12:30 PM	Hunger	20 minutes	Tired and Hungry	Take a break for a snack and set a timer to return to work promptly.
2:00 PM	Phone notification	5 minutes	Distracted and Anxious	Turn off non-essential notifications, schedule a specific time to check your phone, and keep it nearby for emergencies.
3:45 PM	Daydreaming	15 minutes	Bored and Uninterested	Take a short break to stretch, refocus, and return to your task with renewed energy.

Tips for Success

- Be honest with your entries; tracking only works when you acknowledge all distractions.
- Celebrate small victories when you successfully minimize or avoid a distraction!

With the **Distraction Log for Children**, staying focused becomes easier, one step at a time. Let's work together to turn distractions into opportunities for growth!

Distraction Log for Children (Blank)

The Distraction Log for Children is designed to help track and overcome distractions. It includes sections for noting the time, type of distraction, duration, and strategies for improvement. Encourage your child to fill out the log with your guidance in a supportive and non-judgmental way. This tool is meant to improve focus and productivity by raising awareness of distractions and fostering effective strategies to manage them. *(Note: Feel free to customize this template to suit your specific needs.)*

Time of Day	Distraction	Duration	How it Made Me Feel	Strategy to Overcome

For Parents and Teachers: Key Takeaways from Chapter 18

The **Distraction Log** is a practical tool to help children become more aware of what interrupts their focus and develop strategies to stay on track. By tracking distractions throughout the day, they can recognize patterns and take **proactive steps to minimize them**.

Encourage your child to use this log regularly and reflect on their progress. Discuss their findings together, helping them brainstorm realistic solutions. **Your support in guiding these conversations** will empower them to build stronger concentration skills, form better study habits, and develop lifelong time management techniques.

Let them know that overcoming distractions **is a skill that improves with practice**—and that small changes can lead to big improvements in focus and productivity!

Chapter 19

Goal-Setting
Exercise Worksheet

In This Chapter: You'll find **a Goal-Setting Exercise Worksheet** designed to guide children through a comprehensive goal-setting process using the **SMART framework**. Setting clear goals is a key part of effective time management, and our friends Timmy the Tortoise, Bella the Bunny, Max the Monkey, and Lily the Ladybug are here to inspire you on your journey!

Word to Remember: SMART Goals

The **Goal-Setting Exercise Worksheet** will help you define your goals using the **SMART** framework—**S**pecific, **M**easurable, **A**chievable, **R**elevant, and **T**ime-bound—ensuring you stay focused and productive.

Encourage your child to complete this worksheet thoughtfully. It will serve as a personal roadmap for achieving their dreams while managing their time wisely.

Instructions:

1. Print out the Goal-Setting Exercise Worksheet.

2. Follow the instructions on the worksheet to identify your goals and prioritize activities.

3. Note that the worksheet begins on the next page and may extend onto additional pages.

Encourage your child to refer to their completed worksheet regularly. It will serve as a visual reminder of their goals and priorities, helping them stay on track and motivated—just like our friends working together to build their treehouse!

Goal-Setting Exercise Worksheet

Background

- In our fast-paced lives, finding time to think and reflect on our desires and aspirations can feel like a luxury or an unnecessary distraction from the countless tasks we face daily.

- Without clarity on our goals, we lack direction and may find ourselves drifting through life, unable to make meaningful progress.

- Being uncertain about our objectives also makes it difficult to prioritize ourselves and say "no" to others. Without a clear path to follow, we struggle to assert our own needs and desires.

- Setting goals gives our lives purpose and direction. When we know what we want, we can focus our efforts and ask ourselves, "Does this action bring me closer to my goals or take me further away?"

- Remember, "If you don't know what you want, you'll end up with what you get!" So, let's begin this journey of goal-setting and self-discovery.

Instructions:

1. Carve out some time in your hectic routine.

2. Seek out a tranquil location, or perhaps a cozy café, where the distractions of everyday life won't interfere.

3. Reflect on and respond to the following questions!

Part 1- IDEATION (Brainstorming Ideas):

The objective of this exercise is to generate goal ideas and pinpoint 5 concepts that could be transformed into goals.

Instructions:

(i) For each of the two lists below, write down as many ideas as possible—big or small, anything and everything that comes to mind.

(ii) Next, **highlight five ideas** that excite, inspire, or stand out to you as potential goals.

List 1: Your Aspirations

Write down all the things you want to **BE, DO, and HAVE** in the next 1–5 years. Think about your dreams, ambitions, and personal growth.

_____

_____

_____

_____

_____

_____

List 2: Your Non-Negotiables

Write down everything you **DON'T WANT to BE, DO, or HAVE** in the next 1–5 years. This could include habits to break, negative influences to avoid, or paths that don't align with your vision.

_____

_____

_____

_____

_____

_____

Part 2- Refining your Ideas:

Working toward lackluster goals can be a tough grind. That's why we're double-checking your 5 potential goals to ensure they truly excite and motivate you before proceeding.

List Your Top 5 Potential Goals: Choose 5 things you'd like to work on for the upcoming year. You can select from the 5 ideas generated in Part 1 or come up with other ideas you'd like to pursue in the year ahead.	What will achieving this goal mean for YOU? How will it make you FEEL, and how will it change your life?	How EXCITING do you find this goal? Score it out of 10 below
1.		.... / 10
2.		.... / 10
3.		.... / 10
4.		.... / 10
5.		.... / 10

Are you excited? If your excitement score is 8 or higher – congratulations, you've discovered fantastic goals! However, if your excitement score is below 8, you might want to consider what could make that goal more exciting before proceeding with it.

Part 3- Set Your Goals!

Now it's time to choose 3 goals to genuinely focus on. The most effective goals are:

(a) **Aligned with your values.** The more a goal aligns with your inner or core values, the easier it will be to achieve. (Note: You can achieve goals that don't align with your values, but it's usually more challenging and less fulfilling.) Trust your gut instinct in this regard.

(b) **Stated in the positive.** Focus on what you WANT, for example, "I want healthy fingernails" instead of "I want to stop biting my nails." This approach provides you with a clear image to work towards rather than a constant reminder of what you don't want.

(c) **SPECIFIC!** The more specific you are with your goals, the easier it becomes to stay on the right path and ultimately achieve success!

List the 3 Goals You're Committed to Pursuing: Based on your brainstorming and refinement, write 3 goals you're dedicated to achieving. Think about which ones would disappoint you if left unaccomplished.	The Importance of Your Goals (The Benefits): Identify outcomes and reasons for each goal. Grasp the benefits and importance of achieving them.	Set a Target Date: Set an achievable deadline for goals, providing motivation without stress or self-criticism.	Measuring Success: What and how can completion be proven?
1.		Month Year ..../2......	
2.		Month Year ..../2......	
3.		Month Year ..../2......	

Great! Now, let's examine how you can support your own progress towards these goals and identify any potential roadblocks you may encounter along the way.

Part 4: Preparing for Success.

i. Success Accelerators:	ii. Smash those Obstacles:	iii. How can I best advise myself to ensure goal achievement?
What can I start doing, stop doing, do more or less of to help me achieve my goals?	What obstacles might hinder progress? How might you impede your own success?	
_____	_____	_____
_____	_____	_____
_____	_____	_____

Part 5- Taking Action

What is the ONE action you will take for EACH goal in the next month? (That you can start now!)

Write down one action you will take towards each goal in the next month. Break each action down into smaller steps until you can FULLY COMMIT to them. You can do more than one action if you'd like, but make sure to have a minimum of ONE action for each goal.

GOAL 1 Action	_____	By	_____
GOAL 2 Action	_____	By	_____
GOAL 3 Action	_____	By	_____

And finally, What ONE action will I start tomorrow?

_____

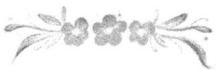

Part 6- Support and Commitment

WHO will support me? Who are my CHEERLEADING TEAM?

Example. Your personal trainer? Coach? Friends? Family? Gym partners? Work colleagues? Be specific on how they can support you

1. Who	_____	HOW Specifically?	_____
2. Who	_____	HOW Specifically?	_____
3. Who	_____	HOW Specifically?	_____

Who will you have to BE to achieve these goals?

_____

☐ **I am committed to achieving my goals Signed** _____

_____

Congratulations! *Take one final step towards committing to your goals by completing the Goal Summary Sheet on the next page.*

Part 7- Take Off!

Ready to take your goals to the next level? Use this Goal Summary Sheet to solidify your commitment:

GOALS SUMMARY SHEET	
YOUR NAME	My **CHEERLEADERS** are: See part 6 1. .... 2. .... 3. ....
My **Goals** are: *See part 3 of this worksheet* 1. I .... by .... 2. I .... by .... 3. I .... by	
The **BENEFITS to me** of my GOALS are: *See part 3 of this worksheet (under The Benefits)* 1. .... 2. .... 3.	My **KEY Action Steps** are: *See part 5 of this worksheet* 1. .... by .... 2. .... by .... 3. .... by .... *Signed:* _____ *Date:* _____
My Success Accelerators: *See part 4 of this worksheet* 1. .... 2. .... 3.	
Thought "Success is not final, failure is not fatal: it is the courage to continue that counts." - Winston Churchill	**TIME MANAGEMENT ADVENTURES**

STAY FOCUSED ON YOUR GOALS!

Cut out the completed Summary Sheet and place it somewhere visible, such as your fridge or bathroom mirror.

For Parents and Teachers: Key Takeaways from Chapter 19

The **Goal-Setting Exercise Worksheet** helps children set clear, actionable goals using the **SMART framework**. Encourage your child to complete it thoughtfully and revisit it regularly as a **roadmap for their progress**.

Discuss their goals with them, celebrate small wins, and guide them in staying focused. With your support, they'll build confidence, stay motivated, and develop strong time management skills!

Chapter 20

Big Rock Exercise: A Productivity & Priorities Tool

In This Chapter: Children will learn to identify and prioritize their most important tasks—their 'Big Rocks'—ensuring they focus on what truly matters. Just like Timmy, Bella, Max, and Lily, under the guidance of Professor Timekeeper, they'll discover how to align their time with their priorities for greater productivity and success.

Word to Remember: BIG ROCKS – Priorities First

Big Rock Exercise: A Productivity & Priorities Tool

Identifying and prioritizing your most important tasks, or "Big Rocks," is an essential part of effective time management. This exercise empowers children to focus on what truly matters by visualizing their priorities and planning their time accordingly. Using the Big Rock Exercise helps ensure that critical tasks are addressed before less significant ones.

Instructions:

1. **Print the Worksheet**: Print out the Big Rock Exercise worksheet provided in this chapter.

2. **Identify Your Big Rocks**: Think about the most important tasks or goals that need your attention and list them under the "Big Rocks" section.

3. **Prioritize Your Tasks**: Rank your tasks based on their significance and urgency, placing the "Big Rocks" at the top.

4. **Plan Accordingly**: Use the space provided to outline how you will allocate time to address your Big Rocks first.

5. **Refer Back Often**: Keep the completed worksheet as a visual reminder of your priorities and to track your progress.

Note: The worksheet spans multiple pages and is designed to help children visualize and consistently align their efforts with their top priorities.

Big Rock Exercise: A Productivity & Priorities Tool

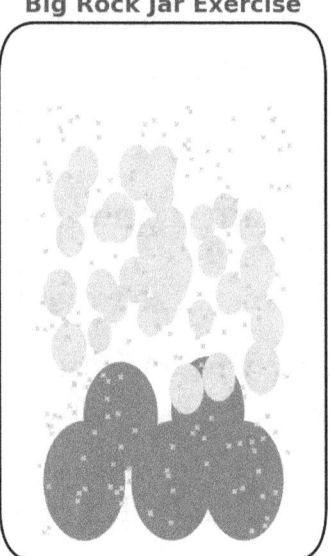

Big Rock Jar Exercise

THE STORY:

A teacher asked his class if a jug filled with big rocks, pebbles, and sand was full. Although the class responded 'yes,' the teacher added pebbles and sand to the jug, showing that the jug wasn't truly full until the big rocks were added first. This story teaches us to prioritize the most important tasks in our lives before filling our time with smaller tasks. This is the concept of the Big Rock exercise, a productivity tool to help us manage our time and focus on what truly matters.

INSTRUCTIONS: Align your time with your priorities by identifying your "Big Rocks" with this exercise. Big Rocks are the most important tasks or goals in your life that align with your values and priorities. Answer the questions, fill in your Big Rocks on the next page, and use what you've learned to make necessary changes on the final page

1. What areas of your life are currently taking up the most of your time? (List everything that comes to mind)

    i. ....

    ii. ....

    iii. ....

    iv. ....

    v. ....

2. What is your current **BIGGEST** time-zapper?

    ....

    (i.e., the negative or unwanted activity that takes up most of your time)

3. What **NEEDS** to change to align your time with your priorities?

....

4. Identify your **top 3 priorities** by reflecting on what's truly important to you in life right now

i. ....

ii. ....

iii. ....

5. Identify the **one thing** that is **most important** to you right

....

Identify & Prioritize Your Rocks!

i. Identify your key priorities or activities in life by listing them on the biggest rocks below.

NOTE: Think carefully about your "Big Rocks" and what is most important to you right now, using the story as a guide?

ii. Fill in the smaller rocks with your next (lower) level of priorities or activities.

iii. Use the remaining spaces (in the tiny gaps between the rocks) for your lowest priorities.

iv. Prioritize your "Big Rocks" by numbering them 1 to 5.

NOTE: Use this tool regularly to prioritize your week or month, and ensure that you schedule your "Big Rocks" first, to align your time with your priorities first!

NEXT: Decide what changes you will make...

Big Rock Jar Exercise

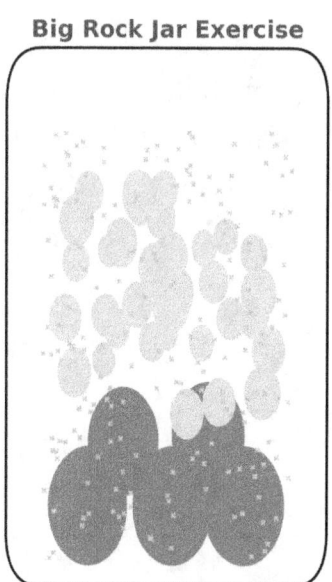

Reflect on your insights from this exercise. What changes will you make to align your time with your priorities and focus on your Big Rocks?

1. How does your current time spent **align** with your "**Big Rocks**," or your **TRUE** priorities in life?

   _____

   _____

2. What have you learned from this exercise?

   _____

   _____

What Needs To Be Changed?

3. What *could* you be doing differently?

   _____

   _____

4. What are the easiest changes you could make to prioritize your time better?	5. What are you WILLING to change to prioritise your time better?	6. Identify potential Obstacles: How you may sabotage yourself? Consider ways to overcome these obstacles to achieve your goals?
_____ _____ _____ _____ _____	_____ _____ _____ _____ _____	_____ _____ _____ _____ _____ _____

What Will You Commit To?

7. Identify three actions you will take to focus on your Big Rocks in life based on the worksheet:

1st Action _____   By when _____
2nd Action _____   By when _____
3rd Action _____   By when _____

Place these action items on post-it notes in visible places like your car, wallet, locker, fridge, or desk to serve as a reminder.

8. Sign and date below to commit to your three actions:

Signed ....   **Date** ....

 What's the **biggest self-discovery** you've made from this exercise?

_____

> "Time is a created thing. To say 'I don't have time,' is like saying, 'I don't want to." - *LaoTzu*

For Parents and Teachers: Key Takeaways from Chapter 20

The **Big Rock Exercise** helps children identify their most important tasks and learn to prioritize effectively. By focusing on their "Big Rocks" first, they can **manage their time wisely and stay on track with their goals**.

Encourage your child to use this worksheet regularly, discuss their priorities with them, and help them balance responsibilities with flexibility. With your guidance, they'll develop **strong decision-making skills and a productivity mindset** that will benefit them for life!

Chapter 21

Blank Prioritization Table

In This Chapter: You'll explore a Blank Prioritization Table—a powerful time management tool designed to help you organize your workload effectively. By focusing on what matters most first, you'll be able to manage your time wisely and achieve your goals with clarity and confidence.

As Timmy, Bella, Max, and Lily worked on their treehouse, they realized that **organizing tasks by importance** made everything smoother and more enjoyable. With Lily's structured lists, the group focused on the **big steps first**, allowing the smaller tasks to naturally fall into place.

Word to Remember: Priority Planner

How to Use the Blank Prioritization Table

The Blank Prioritization Table is your go-to tool for sorting out tasks by importance. It works like a magical map, showing you the way to focus on the most important things first. Follow these steps to make the most of it:

1. **Write Down All Your Tasks**: Start by listing everything you need to do today or this week. Don't worry about the order just yet—just get everything on paper.

2. **Rank the Tasks**: Decide which tasks are most important and label them as **High Priority**. These are the tasks that must be done first.

3. **Identify Medium Priority Tasks**: These are important but can wait until the High Priority tasks are completed.

4. **Label Low Priority Tasks**: These are the tasks you can do later, or even delegate, if possible.

5. **Follow Your Plan**: Start with High Priority tasks and work your way down the list. Keep track of what you've accomplished and celebrate your progress!

Blank Prioritization Table

Task	Priority	Why Is It Important?	Deadline	Done?
	High / Medium / Low			Yes / No
	High / Medium / Low			Yes / No
	High / Medium / Low			Yes / No
	High / Medium / Low			Yes / No
	High / Medium / Low			Yes / No

Example: Prioritization for Treehouse Project

Task	Priority	Why Is It Important?	Deadline	Done?
Measure wood for walls	High	Needed to start building the main structure	Today	Yes
Paint the ladder	Medium	Can wait until the ladder is installed	Tomorrow	No
Decorate the roof	Low	Fun but not essential to finish the treehouse	End of Week	No

Why It Works

By ranking your tasks, you can focus on what matters most and feel less overwhelmed. This approach ensures that you're always making progress on the most important things, while still keeping track of everything else.

Challenge Yourself

As you use the Blank Prioritization Table, try to stick to your plan and complete at least one High Priority task each day. Remember, this is your magical map to staying organized and making the most of your time!

For Parents and Teachers: Key Takeaways from Chapter 21

The **Blank Prioritization Table presented above** directly connects children to **Chapter 2: Setting Priorities – The Treasure Map of Time** and reinforces the importance of prioritization in everyday life. Encourage children to start organizing their tasks and take charge of their time today!

REFLECTION AREA:
•What worked well this week?
•What can I improve next week?
•Did I feel balanced?
TIME CHOREOGRAPHY
Morning
Afternoon
Evening
WEEKLY ROUTINE PLANNER
MORNING
AFTERNOON
EVENING
WEEKLY PLANNER
WEEKLY PLANNER
WEEKLY PLANNER

Chapter 22

Weekly Routine Planner

In This Chapter: With the help of the Weekly Routine Planner, a time management tool, you will design your own schedule and create a week that's balanced, productive, and fun! This tool ties directly to **Chapter 3**: *Creating Routines: The Magic of Daily Rituals*, providing you with the framework to make every week a success.

Words to Remember: Time Choreography and Priority Planner

Time Choreography is the art of intentionally designing and arranging your weekly activities with purpose, balance, and flow—much like a dancer carefully plans and coordinates each movement.

Key Characteristics of Time Choreography

- Deliberate scheduling
- Balanced activity allocation
- Seamless transitions between tasks
- Strategic time management
- Personal rhythm and productivity

Why "Time Choreography" Matters

- Transforms scheduling from a rigid task into a creative process
- Empowers children to view time as a flexible, manageable resource
- Encourages proactive planning
- Makes time management feel engaging and dynamic

Master Your Week: The Priority Planner in Action

During their adventure, the friends in Clocksville discovered the magic of routines. By creating a plan for their week, they found time for everything—building the treehouse, enjoying playtime, and even helping their neighbors.

How to Use the Weekly Routine Planner

1. **List Your Regular Activities**: Write down your school hours, homework, playtime, chores, and any other daily activities.

2. **Add Specific Goals or Tasks**: Include things like finishing a project, practicing a hobby, or spending time with family.

3. **Set Time Blocks**: Allocate specific time slots for each activity. Be realistic about how much time each task takes.

4. **Include Breaks**: Add time to rest, recharge, and enjoy unstructured play.

5. **Review and Adjust**: Check your plan at the end of each day and make changes as needed to stay on track.

Blank Weekly Routine Planner Template

Day	Morning	Afternoon	Evening	Notes/Adjustments
Monday				
Tuesday				
Wednesday				
Thursday				
Friday				
Saturday				
Sunday				

Example: Weekly Routine Filled (Example) for Your Reference

Day	Morning	Afternoon	Evening	Notes/Adjustments
Monday	School	Homework and snack time	Family dinner and reading	Check homework for accuracy

Day	Morning	Afternoon	Evening	Notes/Adjustments
Tuesday	School	Soccer practice	Help with dinner chores	Pack bag for practice tomorrow
Wednesday	School	Art class or hobby time	Watch a family movie	Set out clothes for school
Thursday	School	Finish homework early	Play board games with siblings	Reflect on how the week is going
Friday	School	Relax and play with friends	Pizza night and storytelling	Plan a fun activity for Saturday
Saturday	Morning chores and cartoons	Visit grandparents	Evening walk with family	Adjust based on family plans
Sunday	Attend Sunday school	Do crafts or bake cookies	Prepare school bag for Monday	Plan goals for the next week

Why the Weekly Routine Planner Works

A Weekly Routine Planner helps you see your entire week at a glance, making it easier to balance work, play, and rest. With structure in place, you'll always know what to do next, and you'll feel more in control of your time.

Challenge Yourself

Try using the Weekly Routine Planner for one full week. At the end of the week, reflect on what worked well and what could be improved. Adjust your routine to make the next week even better!

For Parents and Teachers: Key Takeaways from Chapter 22

Time management is a critical life skill that children can learn early with the right support. The Weekly Routine Planner introduces the concept of "Time Choreography" - the art of intentionally designing and arranging activities with purpose, balance, and flow. This tool helps your child develop self-discipline, reduce stress, and build confidence by creating structured yet flexible schedules.

As a parent or teacher, guide your children to use this planner as a tool for personal growth. Encourage them to view time as a flexible, manageable resource. By modeling good time management and providing gentle support, you'll help your child develop executive functioning skills that will benefit them throughout their life. Remember, time management is a learned skill - celebrate progress and help them adjust their routines as needed.

Chapter 23

Task Breakdown Worksheet

In This Chapter: The Task Breakdown Worksheet encourages you to break large tasks into smaller, manageable steps. In one of their biggest lessons from Professor Timekeeper, Timmy, Bella, Max, and Lily learned how to climb the towering **Task Mountain** by breaking big tasks into smaller, manageable steps. This method turned overwhelming challenges into achievable milestones, helping them build their magnificent treehouse one step at a time.

Now, it's your turn to use this strategy for your own tasks using **the Task Breakdown Worksheet—a powerful time management tool!** Whether it's finishing a school project, organizing your room, or preparing for a fun event, this worksheet will help you divide your work into smaller pieces and tackle each step confidently.

During their adventure, the friends in Clocksville discovered how breaking down big tasks makes challenges feel less intimidating and more conquerable.

Word to Remember: Milestone Mapping

Milestone Mapping is the strategic process of breaking complex tasks into smaller, achievable steps that create a clear path to goal completion. It transforms overwhelming challenges into a series of manageable, confidence-building actions.

Milestone Mapping: Key Characteristics

- Breaks down large tasks into bite-sized actions
- Provides clear progression markers
- Reduces overwhelm and anxiety
- Increases motivation through visible progress
- Builds problem-solving skills

Task Breakdown Worksheet

Instructions

1. **Write Down Your Big Task**: Start by identifying the large task you want to complete.

2. **Break It into Smaller Steps**: List the smaller tasks or actions you need to take to complete the big task.

3. **Prioritize the Steps**: Number the smaller steps in the order you need to complete them.

4. **Set Deadlines**: Assign a deadline to each step to stay on track.

5. **Track Your Progress**: Use the "Progress" column to check off each step as you complete it.

Blank Template

Big Task: _____
Step
_____
1. _____
2. _____
3. _____
4. _____
5. _____

Example: Breaking Down a School Science Project

Big Task: Create a Volcano Science Project
Step
1. Research volcano models
2. Buy materials (cardboard, paint, etc.)
3. Build the volcano base
4. Add paint and decorations
5. Prepare the eruption solution

Example: Organizing a Birthday Party

Step	When to Do It	Progress
Decide on the party theme	2 weeks before the party	☑ Completed
Make a guest list	2 weeks before the party	☑ Completed
Send invitations	10 days before the party	☑ Completed
Plan the menu	1 week before the party	☐ In Progress
Buy decorations and supplies	5 days before the party	☐ In Progress
Decorate the venue	1 day before the party	☐ Not Started
Set up the cake and snacks	Day of the party	☐ Not Started
Host the party	Day of the party	☐ Not Started

Why This Tool Works

By breaking large tasks into smaller steps, you'll:

- Feel less overwhelmed.

- Stay organized and focused.

- Celebrate small wins along the way.

So, grab your worksheet, pick a big task, and start breaking it down into manageable steps. You'll be amazed at how much easier—and more fun—it is to accomplish your goals!

For Parents and Teachers: Key Takeaways from Chapter 23

The Task Breakdown Worksheet introduces your child to the powerful concept of Milestone Mapping. This tool empowers children to tackle large, potentially overwhelming tasks by breaking them into smaller, manageable steps. As you support your child in using this worksheet:

1. Encourage them to apply this method to various tasks, from homework to household chores.

2. Celebrate their progress at each milestone to boost confidence and motivation.

3. Help them recognize how this skill reduces anxiety and builds problem-solving abilities.

By mastering Milestone Mapping, your child will develop crucial time management and organizational skills that will serve them well throughout their academic journey and beyond. Remember, your guidance in using this tool can significantly enhance your child's ability to approach challenges with confidence and strategy.

Chapter 24

Calendar or Planner Template

In This Chapter: You'll learn how to use a calendar or planner to schedule your activities and block out time for the things that matter most. This time management tool ties directly to the lessons from **Chapter 5**: *Using a Calendar or Planner: The Time Management Compass*, helping you put your knowledge into practice.

Word to Remember: Time Compass

Time Compass is a strategic approach to navigating daily activities by using planning tools that provide direction, help prioritize tasks, and guide you toward your goals—much like a traditional compass helps travelers find their way.

Time Compass: Key Characteristics

- Provides clear directional guidance for time management
- Helps orient daily activities toward important objectives
- Enables proactive planning
- Reduces decision-making stress
- Creates a sense of control and purpose

Why "Time Compass" Matters

- Transforms scheduling from a passive to an active process
- Empowers individuals to make intentional choices
- Supports goal-oriented time management
- Helps balance responsibilities and personal activities
- Develops strategic thinking skills

The term "Time Compass" directly relates to Professor Timekeeper's analogy in the chapter, making it a meaningful and memorable concept for understanding calendar and planner usage.

Why Use a Calendar or Planner?

Professor Timekeeper explained it best: **"A calendar or planner is like a compass—it keeps you on the right path, guiding you through your day with ease and clarity."** By scheduling your time, you can:

1. **Stay Organized**: Never forget a task or deadline.
2. **Reduce Stress**: Know exactly what you need to do and when.
3. **Maximize Productivity**: Allocate time for priorities and fun activities.

How to Use This Tool

1. **Plan Ahead**: Fill in the calendar or planner with upcoming tasks, activities, and deadlines.
2. **Time Block**: Dedicate specific blocks of time to focus on tasks or goals.
3. **Review and Adjust**: At the end of each day or week, review your progress and adjust as needed.

Calendar or Planner Template

Below are four versions of the template:

1. **Daily Planner**: For detailed time-blocking.
2. **Daily Planner (Blank)**: For you filling your detailed time-blocking.
3. **Weekly Planner**: For a broader view of your week.
4. **Weekly Planner (Blank)**: For you filling a broader view of your week.

Daily Planner Template

Time	Task/Activity	Priority (High/ Medium/Low)	Notes
7:00 AM - 8:00 AM	Morning Routine	Medium	Breakfast, get ready
8:00 AM - 9:00 AM	School Preparation	High	Pack lunch, check supplies

Time	Task/Activity	Priority (High/ Medium/Low)	Notes
9:00 AM - 12:00 PM	School	High	Focus on lessons
12:00 PM - 1:00 PM	Lunch Break	Medium	Relax and recharge
1:00 PM - 3:00 PM	Homework or Projects	High	Focus on priority tasks
3:00 PM - 4:00 PM	Free Play or Relaxation	Low	Enjoy hobbies or rest
4:00 PM - 6:00 PM	Extracurricular Activities	Medium	Sports, art, or practice
6:00 PM - 7:00 PM	Dinner and Family Time	Medium	Share stories, unwind
7:00 PM - 8:00 PM	Review Day and Plan Tomorrow	Medium	Update calendar
8:00 PM - 9:00 PM	Bedtime Routine	High	Prepare for sleep

Daily Planner Template (Blank)

Time	Task/Activity	Priority (High/ Medium/Low)	Notes
7:00 AM - 8:00 AM			
8:00 AM - 9:00 AM			
9:00 AM - 12:00 PM			
12:00 PM - 1:00 PM			
1:00 PM - 3:00 PM			
3:00 PM - 4:00 PM			

Time	Task/Activity	Priority (High/ Medium/Low)	Notes
4:00 PM - 6:00 PM			
6:00 PM - 7:00 PM			
7:00 PM - 8:00 PM			
8:00 PM - 9:00 PM			

Weekly Planner Template

Day	Morning Tasks	Afternoon Tasks	Evening Tasks
Monday	School, assignments	Homework, garden chores	Family time, read a book
Tuesday	Morning routine, school	Piano practice, big rock tasks	Art project
Wednesday	Science experiment, classroom tasks	Homework, outdoor play	Movie night
Thursday	School, review lessons	Group project, prioritize tasks	Relaxation, storytelling
Friday	Reading, class test preparation	Birthday planning, fun tasks	Celebrate, share memories
Saturday	Weekend goals, garden care	Treehouse building, sports	Reflect on progress
Sunday	Morning hike, personal goals	Finish homework, plan the week	Sleep early, set goals

Weekly Planner Template (Blank)

Day	Morning Tasks	Afternoon Tasks	Evening Tasks
Monday			
Tuesday			
Wednesday			
Thursday			
Friday			
Saturday			
Sunday			

Example Use

Lily the Ladybug's Week:

- **Monday**: Focused on finishing her school science project and reserved the evening for watching butterflies in her garden.

- **Tuesday**: Dedicated the morning to helping her friends with the treehouse and blocked out time in the afternoon for practicing her list-making skills.

Reflection Questions

1. Did you stick to your schedule today? If not, why?

2. What changes can you make to your plan to improve tomorrow?

3. Did you achieve your most important tasks? How did it feel?

Practice the blank templates. These tools will help you take control of your time, stay organized, and enjoy every moment of your week!

For Parents and Teachers: Key Takeaways from Chapter 24

The Calendar or Planner Template is an essential tool for teaching children how to manage their time effectively. By introducing this tool early, you help them develop habits that foster organization, responsibility, and balance in their daily lives.

1. **Encourage Regular Use:** Help your child incorporate the calendar into their routine by reviewing it together daily or weekly.

2. **Model Good Practices:** Show them how you use your own calendar to stay organized and prioritize tasks.

3. **Celebrate Progress:** Acknowledge their efforts in maintaining their schedule to build confidence and motivation.

4. **Teach Flexibility:** Remind them that schedules can be adjusted as needed—planning doesn't have to be rigid.

By supporting your child in using this tool consistently, you'll equip them with lifelong skills to stay organized, reduce stress, and achieve their goals while maintaining balance in their lives.

FOCUS CYCLING
WITH THE
POMODORO TECHNIQUE

Task Tracker

- 25 MINUTES FOCUS WORK
- 5 MINUTES BREAK
- REPEAT & REFRESH
- NGER BREAK
  TER 4 SESSIONS

Chapter 25

Pomodoro Timer Chart

In This Chapter: You'll learn about the Pomodoro Technique, a simple yet powerful time management strategy that helps you focus on tasks and maintain energy by working in short bursts with regular breaks. In Chapter 9: *Pomodoro Technique: Work, Rest, Repeat*, Professor Timekeeper explained how this method trains your brain to concentrate while keeping you refreshed.

This Pomodoro Timer Chart is designed to guide you through implementing the Pomodoro Technique for your tasks. By tracking your work and break sessions, you can boost productivity and turn even the toughest tasks into manageable steps.

Word to Remember: Focus Cycling

Focus Cycling is a strategic time management approach that alternates between concentrated work periods and intentional rest breaks, designed to optimize mental performance, prevent burnout, and maintain high productivity.

Focus Cycling: Key Characteristics

- Structured work-break intervals
- Prevents mental fatigue
- Enhances concentration
- Promotes sustainable productivity
- Supports brain's natural attention cycles

Why Use the Pomodoro Timer Chart?

1. **Stay Focused**: Short work sessions help you focus on one task at a time.
2. **Prevent Burnout**: Regular breaks keep your mind fresh and energized.
3. **Track Progress**: See how much you've accomplished in each session.

How to Use This Tool

1. **Choose a Task**: Pick one task to focus on during the work session.
2. **Set a Timer**: Work for 25 minutes (one Pomodoro session).

3. **Take a Break**: Rest for 5 minutes after each session.

4. **Track Progress**: After four sessions, take a longer break (15–30 minutes).

5. **Log Your Work**: Use the chart below to record each session and your progress.

Pomodoro Timer Chart Template

Task Name	Pomodoro Sessions	Breaks	Notes	Status (Done/ In Progress)
Math Homework	🕐 🕐 🕐 🕐	✓ ✓ ✓ 🕐	Focused on algebra problems	Done
Science Project	🕐 🕐 🕐	✓ ✓	Worked on building the model	In Progress
Reading Assignment	🕐 🕐	✓	Completed chapters 4–6	Done
Art Practice	🕐 🕐 🕐	✓ ✓	Painted the background	In Progress
Treehouse Ladder Build	🕐 🕐 🕐 🕐 🕐	✓ ✓ ✓	Finished constructing the ladder	Done

Example Use: Building the Treehouse

Task Name: Treehouse Walls

- **Pomodoro Sessions**: 🕐 🕐 🕐 🕐
- **Breaks**: ✓ ✓ ✓ ✓
- **Notes**: Focused on measuring and cutting wooden panels. Took breaks to stretch and hydrate.
- **Status**: In Progress

Reflection Questions

1. Were you able to stay focused during each session? Why or why not?

2. Did the breaks help you feel refreshed and ready to continue?

3. How can you improve your next Pomodoro session?

Benefits of the Pomodoro Timer Chart

- **Accountability**: Track your time and see your progress.

- **Motivation**: Celebrate completing each Pomodoro session.

- **Flexibility**: Apply this method to any task, big or small.

By practicing the Pomodoro Technique with this chart, you'll gain confidence in managing your time, staying focused, and achieving your goals!

For Parents and Teachers: Key Takeaways from Pomodoro Technique Chapter

The Pomodoro Technique offers a transformative approach to time management that can help children develop critical focus and self-regulation skills. By teaching your child to work in structured, intentional intervals, you're helping them learn to manage attention, reduce overwhelm, and build sustainable productivity habits.

Encourage your child to experiment with this technique, recognizing that learning to focus is a skill that develops over time. Support them by creating a distraction-free environment, helping them set realistic work intervals, and celebrating their progress in managing tasks more effectively. Remember, the goal is not perfection, but gradual improvement in concentration and time management skills.

Chapter 26

Deep Work Checklist

In This Chapter: You'll learn about Deep Work, a key tool for achieving great things. By focusing on one important task without distractions, you can give your best effort and see amazing results. In Chapter 10: *Deep Work: Focus Like a Champion*, Professor Timekeeper taught the friends how to immerse themselves fully in their tasks, comparing it to diving deep into the ocean to find hidden treasures.

This Deep Work Checklist is designed to help you prepare for and execute distraction-free, focused work sessions. It's a simple guide to ensure you're ready to dive deep and succeed.

Word to Remember: Focus Immersion

Focus Immersion is the practice of dedicating uninterrupted time and attention to a single, important task or subject, allowing for deep concentration and maximum productivity.

Focus Immersion: Key Characteristics:

- Eliminates distractions
- Promotes deep thinking and problem-solving
- Enhances creativity and innovation
- Improves quality of work
- Increases efficiency and productivity

By mastering Focus Immersion, you can tackle complex tasks more effectively and achieve higher levels of understanding and accomplishment in your work or studies.

Why Use the Deep Work Checklist?

1. **Minimize Distractions**: Set up your environment for success.
2. **Enhance Focus**: Commit fully to the task at hand.
3. **Build Discipline**: Practice deep work as a powerful skill for the future.

How to Use This Tool

1. **Prepare Your Environment**: Follow the checklist to remove distractions and set up a workspace that helps you focus.

2. **Start Deep Work**: Use the checklist to guide you through each step of your session.

3. **Reflect**: After your session, review what went well and what could improve.

Deep Work Checklists

The following are two Deep Work Checklists:

1. Deep Work Checklist with an Example

2. Deep Work Checklist (Blank) for Practice

Deep Work Checklist (with an Example)

Step 1: Before You Begin
- **Choose a Single Task**: What's the most important task you need to focus on?
- **Set a Time Limit**: Decide how long you'll work (e.g., 30 minutes, 1 hour).
- **Find a Quiet Workspace**: Pick a spot where you won't be interrupted.
- **Turn Off Distractions**:
    o   Silence your phone or place it in another room.
    o   Close unnecessary apps, tabs, or devices.
- **Gather Supplies**: Have everything you need (e.g., books, pens, water).

Step 2: During Deep Work
- **Set a Timer**: Track the time you plan to work.
- **Stay Focused**: If your mind wanders, gently bring it back to the task.
- **Take Short Notes**: If you think of unrelated ideas, jot them down to address later.

- **Use Positive Reminders**: Repeat phrases like, "I can do this" or "Stay focused."

Step 3: After Your Session

- **Celebrate Your Progress**: Write down what you accomplished.
- **Reflect**:
    - o   What worked well during this session?
    - o   Were there distractions? How can you manage them next time?
- **Plan the Next Session**: What's the next step for your task?

Deep Work Checklist (Blank) for Practice

Checklist Step	Details
Step 1: Before You Begin	
☐ Choose a Single Task	
☐ Set a Time Limit	
☐ Find a Quiet Workspace	
☐ Turn Off Distractions	
☐ Gather Supplies	
Step 2: During Deep Work	
☐ Set a Timer	
☐ Stay Focused	
☐ Take Short Notes	
☐ Use Positive Reminders	

Checklist Step	Details
Step 3: After Your Session	
☐ Celebrate Your Progress	
☐ Reflect	
☐ Plan the Next Session	

Example: Deep Work for a Science Project

- **Task:** Writing the hypothesis for the science project.

- **Time:** 45 minutes.

- **Environment:** At the study desk with a notebook, pen, and no devices nearby.

- **Progress:** Completed the draft and organized the research notes.

- **Reflection:** Staying off my phone helped me stay focused. I'll use this strategy next time.

Tips for Success

- **Start small:** Aim for 20–30 minutes of deep work and gradually increase the duration.

- **Be consistent:** Practice deep work regularly to build focus as a habit.

- **Reward yourself:** After completing your session, take a break or enjoy a small treat.

Benefits of Using the Deep Work Checklist

- **Improved Focus:** Stay committed to your tasks.

- **Higher Productivity:** Achieve more in less time.

- **Sense of Accomplishment:** Feel proud of what you've completed.

By using this checklist, you'll unlock the power of deep work and achieve incredible results, just like Timmy, Bella, Max, and Lily did!

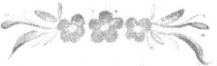

For Parents and Teachers: Key Takeaways from Deep Work Chapter

Deep Work is more than a productivity technique—it's a critical skill that helps children develop focus, resilience, and the ability to tackle complex challenges. By introducing your child to intentional, distraction-free work sessions, you're equipping them with a powerful strategy to navigate an increasingly fragmented digital world.

Encourage your child to create dedicated, interruption-free work environments and model focused behavior in your own tasks. Help them understand that deep concentration is a skill that improves with practice, teaching them to value quality of work over mere busyness. Your support in developing this skill can significantly enhance their learning, creativity, and future success.

Chapter 27

20/80 Task Chart

In this chapter: We explore the Pareto Principle, often called the **80/20 Rule,** which reveals that 80% of our results typically come from just 20% of our efforts. Using this powerful tool, you'll learn to identify and focus on your most impactful tasks, achieving more in less time. It's all about working smarter, not harder!

What is the 20/80 Rule?

The 20/80 Rule is a game-changing way to think about priorities:

- 20% of your tasks often bring 80% of your success.

- By focusing on what matters most, you can maximize your efforts and achievements.

Word to Remember: Impact Focus

Impact Focus is the practice of identifying and prioritizing the tasks or activities that yield the most significant results, allowing you to achieve more with less effort.

Impact Focus: Key Characteristics:

- Emphasizes quality over quantity in task selection

- Encourages strategic thinking about priorities

- Boosts efficiency and productivity

- Reduces time spent on less impactful activities

- Helps achieve better results with less stress

By mastering Impact Focus, you learn to direct your energy towards what truly matters, making the most of your time and talents.

How to Use the 20/80 Task Chart

This chart helps you identify high-impact tasks and organize your time around them. Follow these steps to get started:

1. **List Your Tasks:** Write down everything you need to do.

2. **Evaluate Impact:** For each task, ask:
   o   Will this bring me closer to my goal?
   o   How much does this task matter compared to others?

3. **Highlight High-Impact Tasks:** Mark the top 20% of tasks that will give you 80% of the results.

4. **Focus First:** Start with the high-impact tasks before moving to the rest.

5. **Reflect and Adjust:** At the end of the day or week, think about how focusing on the 20% helped you.

20/80 Task Chart Example: Preparing for a School Science Project

Tasks	Impact Level (Low, Medium, High)	High-Impact Task (✓)?
Research project ideas	High	✓
Create project outline	High	✓
Design experiment setup	Medium	
Purchase materials	Low	
Write the final report	High	✓
Create display board	Medium	
Practice presentation	High	✓

Reflection Example

"By focusing on the **Research Project Ideas, Outline, Final Report**, and **Presentation**, I made huge progress. These were the tasks that really mattered for my science project success!"

Why It Works

- Keeps you from wasting time on low-impact tasks.

- Helps you prioritize and stay on track.

- Encourages focus on the most meaningful work.

Practice Time!

Now it's your turn! Use the blank **20/80 Task Chart** below to apply the Pareto Principle to your tasks.

Tasks	Impact Level (Low, Medium, High)	High-Impact Task (✓)?

Key Takeaways

- Small, focused efforts lead to big results.

- Use the **20/80 Task Chart** regularly to build your prioritization skills.

- Practice makes perfect—over time, identifying your top 20% will become second nature.

For Parents and Teachers: Key Takeaways from Chapter 27

The 20/80 Task Chart introduces your child to a powerful principle for prioritizing and focusing their efforts. As you guide your child in using this tool:

- Help them identify their most impactful tasks or activities.

- Encourage them to allocate more time and energy to these high-value tasks.

- Discuss how this approach can reduce stress and increase productivity.

- Model the use of this principle in your own life and work.

By mastering the 20/80 rule, your child will develop crucial skills in time management, decision-making, and strategic thinking. Remember, the goal is to work smarter, not harder. Your support in applying this principle can significantly enhance your child's ability to prioritize effectively and achieve better results in school and beyond.

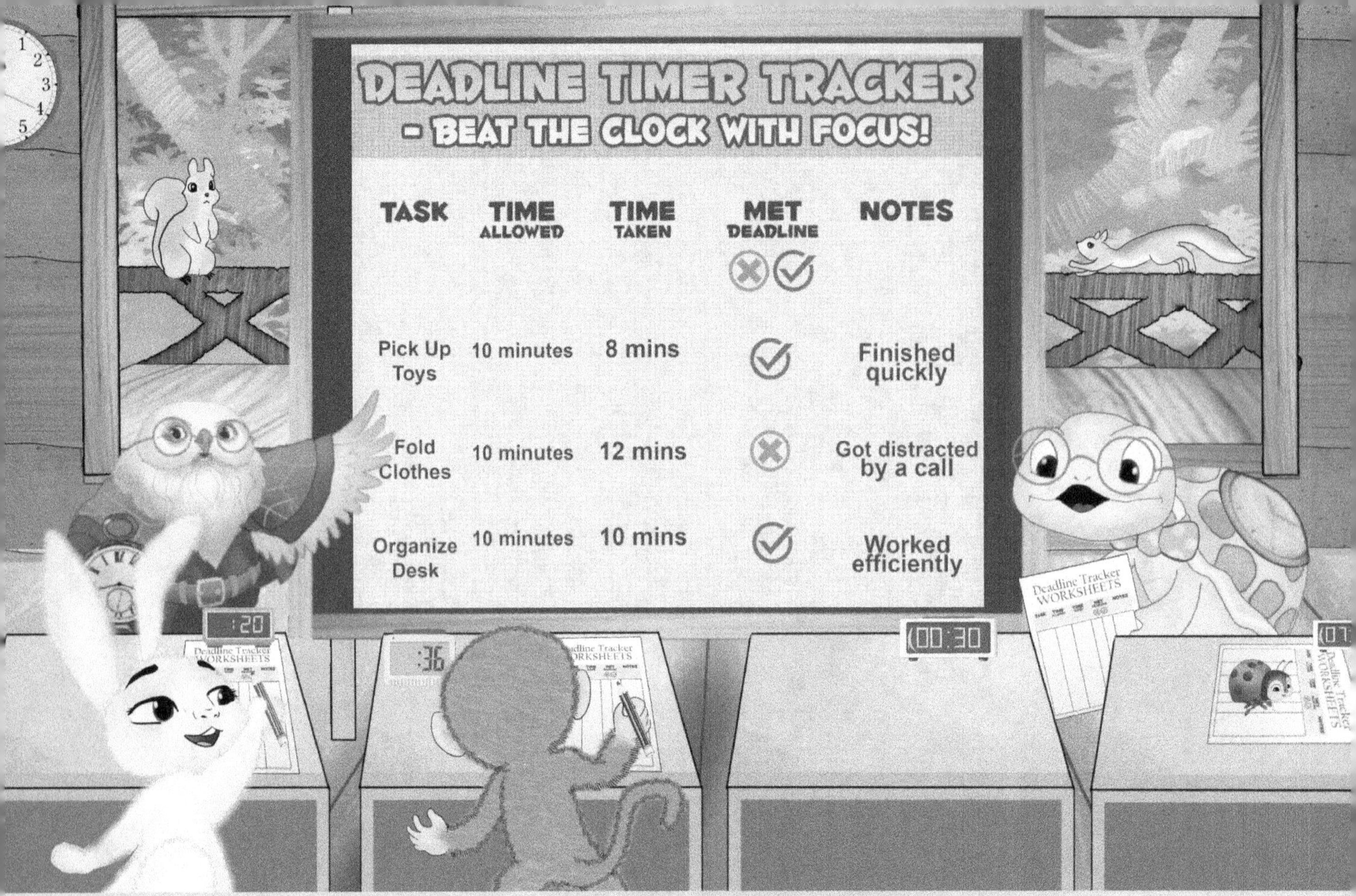

DEADLINE TIMER TRACKER
– BEAT THE CLOCK WITH FOCUS!

TASK	TIME ALLOWED	TIME TAKEN	MET DEADLINE ✗ ✓	NOTES
Pick Up Toys	10 minutes	8 mins	✓	Finished quickly
Fold Clothes	10 minutes	12 mins	✗	Got distracted by a call
Organize Desk	10 minutes	10 mins	✓	Worked efficiently

Chapter 28

Deadline Timer Tracker

In This Chapter: You'll learn about the power of deadlines as motivators and how to use them effectively. We introduce the **Deadline Timer Tracker**, a tool to set realistic time limits for your tasks and measure how effectively you meet them. This simple yet effective method helps beat procrastination and improves time management skills.

Why Deadlines Work

Deadlines help by:
1. **Focusing Your Efforts:** When you know the clock is ticking, you're less likely to waste time.

2. **Breaking Procrastination:** Deadlines create a sense of urgency, making it easier to start tasks.

3. **Encouraging Efficiency:** Knowing you have a limited amount of time helps you streamline your work.

Words to Remember: Time Anchors and Deadlines

Time Anchor is a self-imposed deadline or time limit that helps ground your focus, motivate action, and improve task completion efficiency.

Key Characteristics of Time Anchor:

- Creates a sense of urgency

- Provides a clear target for task completion

- Helps prioritize and focus efforts

- Reduces procrastination

- Improves time estimation skills

Deadline, on the other hand, refers to a specific point in time by which a task must be completed. While deadlines can sometimes feel restrictive, they serve as important motivators that encourage productivity and help you manage your time effectively.

Key Characteristics of Deadline:

- Imposes a clear end point for tasks

- Instills a sense of urgency

- Drives accountability and responsibility

- Can help break large projects into manageable parts

By understanding both Time Anchors and Deadlines, you can develop a more comprehensive approach to time management. Use Time Anchors to set personal limits that guide your work, while also recognizing the importance of external deadlines in keeping you on track. Together, these concepts will empower you to manage your time more effectively and achieve your goals with greater ease.

How to Use the Deadline Timer Tracker

The **Deadline Timer Tracker** works by dividing tasks into time blocks and tracking your progress. Follow these steps:

1. **Choose a Task:** Pick a task you need to complete.

2. **Set a Deadline:** Decide how much time you'll spend on it. Be realistic but firm.

3. **Use a Timer:** Use a stopwatch, timer, or app to track your time.

4. **Monitor Progress:** Note how close you came to meeting your deadline.

5. **Reflect and Adjust:** At the end of the session, reflect on what worked and what didn't.

Example of Deadline Timer Tracker: Cleaning Your Room in 30 Minutes

Task	Time Allowed	Time Taken	Met Deadline? (✓/✗)	Notes
Pick up toys	10 minutes	8 minutes	✓	Finished quickly, no distractions.

Task	Time Allowed	Time Taken	Met Deadline? (✓/✗)	Notes
Fold clothes	10 minutes	12 minutes	✗	Got distracted by a phone call.
Organize desk	10 minutes	10 minutes	✓	Stayed focused and worked efficiently.

Reflection Example

"By setting a 30-minute deadline, I stayed on track. Even though I missed one, I was able to finish my room faster than usual!"

Why It Works

- **Builds Awareness:** Shows how long tasks take and where you might need to improve.

- **Encourages Focus:** Reduces distractions by creating a time limit.

- **Improves Time Estimation Skills:** Helps you set realistic deadlines for future tasks.

Practice Time!

Use the blank **Deadline Timer Tracker** below for your tasks today.

Task	Time Allowed	Time Taken	Met Deadline? (✓/✗)	Notes

Task	Time Allowed	Time Taken	Met Deadline? (✓/✗)	Notes

Tips for Success

- **Start Small:** Begin with short tasks to build confidence.

- **Reward Yourself:** Celebrate when you meet deadlines.

- **Learn from Missed Deadlines:** Analyze what went wrong and adjust.

Key Takeaways

- Deadlines help you stay productive and efficient.

- The **Deadline Timer Tracker** makes setting and meeting deadlines fun and rewarding.

- Practice using this tool daily to master the art of working within time limits.

For Parents and Teachers: Key Takeaways from Chapter 28

The Deadline Timer Tracker introduces your child to effective time management using deadlines and self-imposed time limits. As you support your child in using this tool:

1. Help them set realistic deadlines for tasks, breaking larger projects into smaller, timed segments.

2. Encourage the use of visual timers to make time more tangible and help with pacing.

3. Teach them to prioritize tasks and create schedules, balancing work with breaks.

4. Model good time management practices by sharing your own strategies and experiences.

5. Celebrate their progress in meeting deadlines and reflect on areas for improvement.

By mastering the concepts of Time Anchors and Deadlines, your child will develop crucial skills in time estimation, task prioritization, and efficient work habits. This foundation will serve them well in academic pursuits and beyond, fostering independence and reducing stress associated with time management.

Chapter 29

Frog Task Tracker

In This Chapter: You'll learn about **Frog Task Tracker**, a tool to help you identify, prioritize, and tackle your frogs first thing in the day. This practice will help you overcome procrastination and build momentum for the rest of your tasks.

Have you ever had a task that felt so big or difficult that you kept avoiding it? That's your "**frog**"—your hardest or most important task.

Word to Remember: Frog Task

Frog Task refers to the most challenging or important task of the day that should be prioritized and completed first to boost productivity and overcome procrastination.

Key characteristics of a Frog Task:

- Often the most difficult or daunting task on your to-do list
- Typically has high importance or impact
- Requires focused effort and concentration
- When completed early, provides a sense of accomplishment and momentum for the rest of the day

By identifying and tackling your Frog Task first, you can improve your productivity and reduce the tendency to procrastinate on important work.

Why Tackle Your Frog First?

1. **Eliminates Procrastination:** Starting with the hardest task clears the biggest obstacle from your day.

2. **Builds Confidence:** Completing a challenging task first gives you a sense of accomplishment.

3. **Frees Mental Space:** Once your frog is done, the rest of the day feels lighter and easier.

How to Use the Frog Task Tracker

This tool guides you through identifying and conquering your daily frogs.

Follow these steps:
1. **Identify Your Frog:** Write down the hardest or most important task you need to do.
2. **Set a Deadline:** Decide when you'll tackle your frog (e.g., first thing in the morning).
3. **Track Progress:** Use the tracker to record when you completed the task and how you felt afterward.
4. **Reflect:** Think about what helped you succeed and what you can improve next time.

Example: Frog Task Tracker in Action

Date	Frog Task	Why It's Important	Deadline	Completed? (✓/✗)	How Did I Feel?
March 1	Finish science project	It's due tomorrow, and I want a good grade.	9:00 AM	✓	Proud! I feel ready for the next task.
March 2	Clean my messy desk	I need a tidy space to focus on homework.	8:30 AM	✓	Relieved and energized.
March 3	Practice my presentation	I'm nervous, but practicing will help me feel confident.	7:45 AM	✗	Felt distracted— will try again tomorrow.

Tips for Success

1. **Start Small:** If your frog feels too big, break it into smaller steps using the **Task Breakdown Worksheet**.

2. **Use Positive Rewards:** Celebrate after completing your frog with a fun activity or treat.

3. **Stay Consistent:** Make tackling your frog a daily habit.

Practice Time!

Use the blank **Frog Task Tracker** below to plan and conquer your frogs for the week.

Date	Frog Task	Why It's Important	Deadline	Completed? (✓/✗)	How Did I Feel?

Why This Tool Works

- **Encourages Prioritization:** Helps you identify and focus on what matters most.

- **Builds Momentum:** Tackling the hardest task first boosts productivity for the rest of your day.

- **Promotes Self-Reflection:** Reflecting on your feelings after completing tasks fosters growth and resilience.

Key Takeaways

- Start your day by "eating your frog"—tackling your hardest or most important task.

- Use the **Frog Task Tracker** to stay accountable and track your progress.

- Practice this habit daily to unlock your full potential and make every day more productive.

For Parents and Teachers: Key Takeaways from Chapter 29

The Frog Task Tracker introduces a powerful strategy for overcoming procrastination and building productive habits. By teaching your child to identify and tackle their most challenging task first, you're helping them develop:

1. Resilience in facing difficult challenges

2. Confidence through early task completion

3. Strategic thinking about task prioritization

4. Momentum for daily productivity

Support your child by helping them recognize their "frog" tasks and creating an environment that encourages tackling challenging work early.

Chapter 30

Time Management Reflection Journal

In this chapter, You'll learn about the **Time Management Reflection Journal**, a tool designed to help you evaluate your daily and weekly practices, notice and honor your achievements, and identify areas for growth. Reflection is the key to continuous improvement and mastering your time management skills.

Time management isn't just about planning and completing tasks—it's also about reflecting on your progress and learning from your experiences.

Word to Remember: Time Reflection

Time Reflection is the practice of regularly reviewing and analyzing how you use your time, acknowledging successes, identifying areas for improvement, and adjusting your strategies to enhance productivity and personal growth.

Key aspects of Time Reflection:

- Evaluates daily and weekly time management practices
- Celebrates achievements and progress
- Identifies patterns and areas for improvement
- Promotes continuous learning and adaptation
- Enhances self-awareness about time usage

By engaging in Time Reflection, you develop a deeper understanding of your time management habits and can make more informed decisions about how to allocate your time and energy effectively.

Why Reflect on Time Management?

1. **Learn from Experience:** Understand what worked well and what didn't.
2. **Celebrate Successes:** Acknowledge your achievements to stay motivated.
3. **Identify Growth Areas:** Pinpoint habits or strategies that need adjustment.
4. **Build Self-Awareness:** Develop a deeper understanding of how you use your time.

How to Use the Time Management Reflection Journal

This journal can be used daily or weekly to assess your time management habits. Each entry includes guided prompts to help you think critically about your time usage.

Daily Reflection Prompts

1. What did I accomplish today?

2. What went well with my time management?

3. What challenges did I face, and how did I handle them?

4. What will I do differently tomorrow to improve?

Example: Daily Reflection Table

Date	Accomplishments	What Went Well?	Challenges	Improvement Plan
March 1	Finished math homework and cleaned room	Stayed focused with Pomodoro breaks	Got distracted by my phone	Turn off phone notifications tomorrow.
March 2	Completed science project	Prioritized tasks with my planner	Felt tired in the afternoon	Take a 10-minute walk for energy.

Weekly Reflection Prompts

1. What were my biggest accomplishments this week?

2. Which time management tools helped me the most?

3. Did I meet my goals? Why or why not?

4. What's one new strategy I want to try next week?

Example: Weekly Reflection Table

Week Ending	Accomplishments	Tools That Helped	Goals Met? (Yes/No)	New Strategy to Try
March 5	Finished project, practiced presentation	Planner, Task Breakdown Worksheet	Yes	Start using the Frog Task Tracker.
March 12	Stayed ahead on homework	Distraction Log, Pomodoro Timer Chart	No (missed one goal)	Schedule shorter, focused sessions.

Customizing Your Reflection Journal

- **Add Personal Goals:** Include spaces to track personal goals or habits.

- **Include Positive Affirmations:** End each entry with a positive note about your progress.

- **Use Creative Elements:** Encourage creativity with drawings, stickers, or colors to make reflection enjoyable.

Why This Tool Works

1. **Promotes Accountability:** Reflecting regularly keeps you accountable to your goals.

2. **Encourages Growth:** Identifying patterns helps you improve your strategies.

3. **Builds Confidence:** Acknowledging progress boosts self-esteem and motivation.

Example: Reflection Journal Entry

Date	Accomplishments	What Went Well?	Challenges	Improvement Plan
March 3	Finished art project, cleaned desk	Focused on tasks with time blocking	Overwhelmed by too many tasks	Use Prioritization Table tomorrow.

Week Ending	Accomplishments	Tools That Helped	Goals Met? (Yes/No)	New Strategy to Try
March 10	Completed assignments early	Planner, Big Rock Exercise	Yes	Experiment with Deep Work sessions.

Key Takeaways

- Use the **Time Management Reflection Journal** to reflect daily and weekly.

- Celebrate your wins, analyze challenges, and plan improvements.

- Reflection is the bridge between where you are and where you want to be.

For Parents and Teachers: Key Takeaways from Chapter 30

The Time Management Reflection Journal is a powerful tool that teaches children the critical skill of self-assessment and continuous improvement. By encouraging regular reflection, you help your child:

1. Develop self-awareness about their time management habits

2. Learn from both successes and challenges

3. Build metacognitive skills that support lifelong learning

4. Create a growth mindset approach to personal development

Support your child by:
- Setting aside consistent time for reflection

- Asking open-ended questions about their experiences

- Celebrating their insights and growth

- Modeling reflective practices in your own life

Remember, reflection is not about perfection, but about understanding, learning, and progressively improving time management skills.

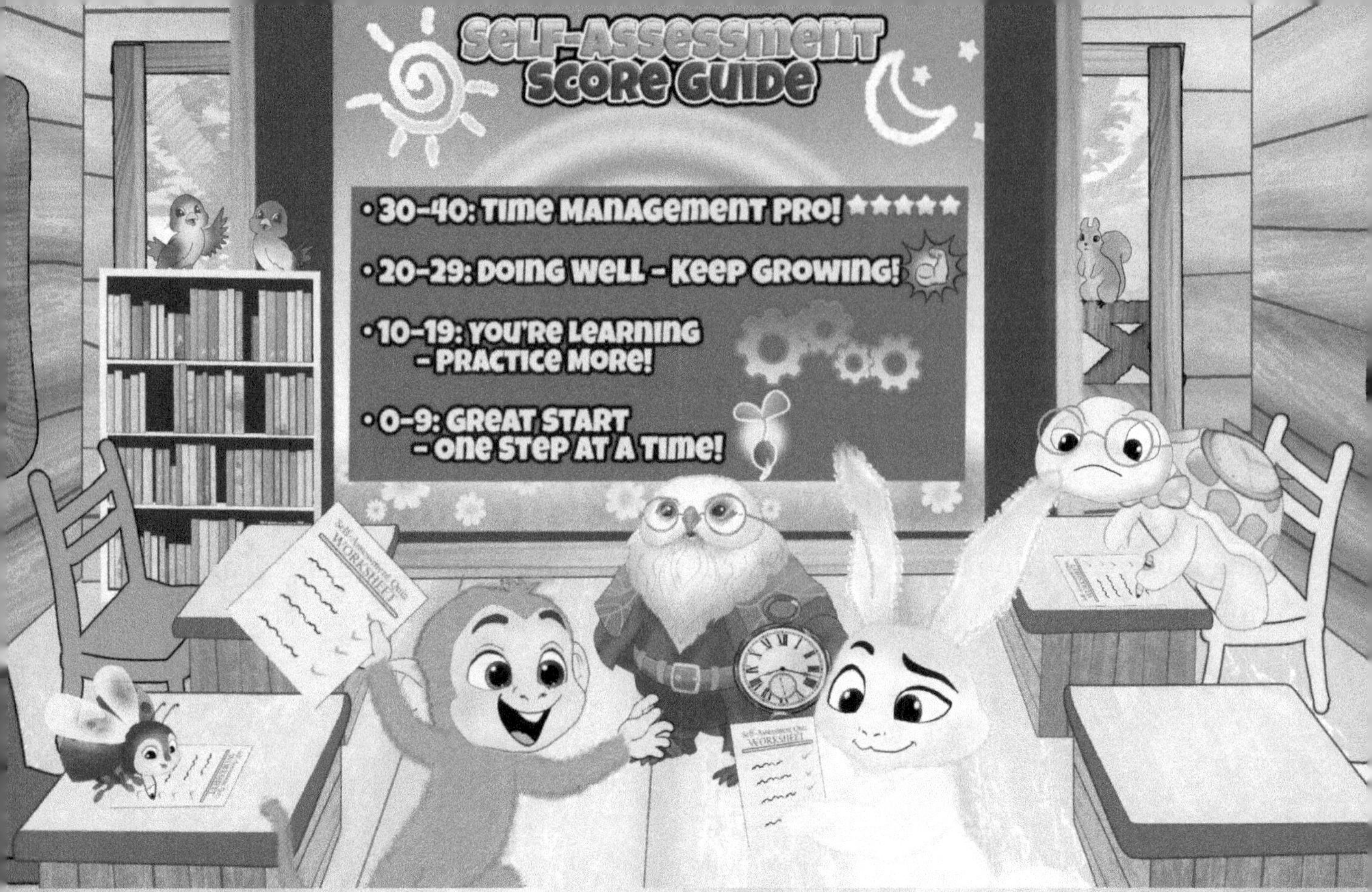

- **30–40: TIME MANAGEMENT PRO!** ★★★★★
- **20–29: DOING WELL – KEEP GROWING!**
- **10–19: YOU'RE LEARNING – PRACTICE MORE!**
- **0–9: GREAT START – ONE STEP AT A TIME!**

Chapter 31

Self-Assessment
Quiz Worksheet

In this chapter, you'll expand your learning on the concepts from the **Time Management Self-Assessment Quiz** by exploring a detailed, interactive worksheet. This tool allows you to evaluate your habits and skills in greater depth, giving you actionable insights to improve your time management.

Self-assessment is a powerful way to understand your strengths and areas for growth in time management.

Word to Remember: Self-Awareness

How to Use the Self-Assessment Quiz Worksheet

1. Complete the questions honestly.

2. Use the scoring guide to understand your current time management skills.

3. Reflect on your results and identify areas for improvement.

4. Take action using the suggestions provided for each section.

Self-Assessment Quiz Worksheet

Part 1: Daily Habits and Routines

Rate yourself on each statement below using this scale:
1 = Never | 2 = Sometimes | 3 = Often | 4 = Always

Statement	Score
I follow a consistent daily routine.	
I plan my day the night before.	
I prioritize the most important tasks first.	
I take regular breaks to stay energized.	
I finish tasks I start without procrastinating.	

Total Score for Part 1: _____

Part 2: Tools and Strategies

Rate yourself on how often you use the following time management tools:

Tool or Strategy	Score
I use a calendar or planner to track tasks.	
I break large tasks into smaller steps.	
I set deadlines for my tasks.	
I use prioritization techniques, like the Big Rock Exercise.	
I minimize distractions during focused work.	

Total Score for Part 2: _____

Part 3: Reflection and Adaptability

Rate yourself on how well you reflect and adapt to challenges:

Statement	Score
I reflect on what went well and what didn't after completing tasks.	
I adjust my plans when unexpected events happen.	
I ask for help when I need it.	
I can quickly refocus after being interrupted.	
I track my progress toward long-term goals.	

Total Score for Part 3: _____

Scoring Guide

Add up your total score for all sections:

Score Range	Interpretation
46-60 points	Excellent time management skills. Keep up the great work!
31-45 points	Good time management skills, but there's room to improve.
16-30 points	Fair time management skills. Focus on building stronger habits.
0-15 points	Needs improvement. Start by mastering one skill at a time.

Actionable Insights by Section

Part 1: Daily Habits and Routines

- If you scored low, start by creating a daily routine using the **Weekly Routine Planner** (Chapter 22).

- Use the **Pomodoro Timer Chart** (Chapter 25) to develop focused work habits.

Part 2: Tools and Strategies

- Struggling with organization? Try the **Calendar or Planner Template** (Chapter 24).

- Improve task management with the **Task Breakdown Worksheet** (Chapter 23).

Part 3: Reflection and Adaptability

- Use the **Time Management Reflection Journal** (Chapter 30) to build self-awareness.

- Practice flexibility with the **Prioritization Table** (Chapter 21) to adapt to changes.

Example Entry

Part	Statement or Tool	Score
Part 1	I follow a consistent daily routine.	3
Part 2	I use a calendar or planner to track tasks.	4
Part 3	I reflect on what went well and what didn't.	2

Total Score: 27/60 (Assume you completed all questions in all parts; this places you in the 'Fair' range).

Interpretation:

- Good time management skills with room for improvement. Focus on creating a consistent daily routine and building reflection habits.

Why This Worksheet Works

- **Holistic Evaluation:** Covers routines, tools, and reflection for a comprehensive assessment.

- **Actionable Insights:** Provides clear next steps based on your score.

- **Interactive Design:** Engages users with a hands-on approach to self-improvement.

For Parents and Teachers: Key Takeaways from Chapter 31

The Self-Assessment Quiz Worksheet is a valuable tool for developing your child's self-awareness and critical thinking skills in relation to time management. As you guide your child through this process:

1. Encourage honest self-reflection without judgment.

2. Help them identify patterns in their responses.

3. Discuss how their self-assessment aligns with your observations.

4. Guide them in setting specific, achievable goals based on their results.

5. Revisit the assessment periodically to track progress and adjust strategies.

By mastering self-assessment, your child will develop valuable skills for lifelong learning and personal growth.

Support your child's journey by modeling self-reflection and discussing your own time management strategies and challenges.

This open dialogue will reinforce the importance of self-awareness and continuous improvement in all aspects of life.

Chapter 32

Self-Assessment Results and Improvement Tracker

In This Chapter: You'll learn to interpret your results and create a personalized plan to improve your time management skills. With the **Improvement Tracker**, you can turn insights into action and watch your progress grow over time.

Congratulations on completing the Self-Assessment Quiz from the previous chapter! As the final chapter of this time management journey, this represents more than just a conclusion—it's a beginning. Among the comprehensive toolkit of strategies, techniques, and insights you've learned to transform your approach to time management, the key steps for using the Self-Assessment Results and Improvement Tracker include:

- Interpreting Your Results
- Creating Your Personalized Plan
- Reflecting and Adjusting
- Using the Improvement Tracker for Growth

Word to Remember: Growth Mindset

Growth Mindset is the belief that your abilities and skills can be developed through dedication, hard work, and continuous learning.

Key Characteristics of Growth Mindset:

- Embraces challenges as opportunities
- Views mistakes as learning experiences
- Believes in continuous improvement
- Encourages persistent effort
- Transforms potential limitations into strengths

How to Use the Results and Improvement Tracker

1. **Understand Your Score**: Use the scoring guide from Chapter 31 to identify your current skill level.

2. **Set Goals for Growth**: Based on your results, decide which areas to improve first.

3. **Track Your Progress**: Use the tracker to monitor your actions and reflect on what's working.

4. **Celebrate Milestones**: Acknowledge and reward yourself for improvements along the way.

Step 1: Interpreting Your Results

Review your total and section scores from the quiz:

Score Range	Interpretation
46-60 points	Excellent time management skills. Keep refining and practicing!
31-45 points	Good skills, but focus on strengthening specific areas.
16-30 points	Needs improvement. Prioritize building foundational habits.
0-15 points	Significant improvement needed. Start with small, achievable steps.

Step 2: Create Your Personalized Plan

Use this table to identify areas for improvement and set SMART goals.

Area for Improvement	Specific Goal	Action Plan	Timeline	Progress
Example: Daily Routine	Create and follow a daily routine for 2 weeks.	Use the Weekly Routine Planner (Chapter 22).	Start today.	Track progress daily.
Example: Managing Distractions	Reduce distractions during homework.	Turn off my phone and use the Distraction Log (Chapter 18).	1 week to practice.	Reflect every evening.

Blank Personalized Plan template

Area for Improvement	Specific Goal	Action Plan	Timeline	Progress

Step 3: Improvement Tracker

The tracker helps you stay consistent and identify what's working.

Date	Focus Area	Action Taken	Success? (Y/N)	Notes/Reflection
Day 1	Managing Distractions	Turned off my phone for 1 hour.	Yes	Felt more focused; will try again tomorrow.
Day 2	Breaking Tasks into Steps	Used the Task Breakdown Worksheet.	Yes	Easier to complete tasks; very helpful!

Blank Improvement Tracker Template

Date	Focus Area	Action Taken	Success? (Y/N)	Notes/Reflection

Step 4: Reflect and Adjust

Every week, review your Improvement Tracker and ask yourself:

1. What worked well this week?

2. What challenges did I face, and how can I address them?

3. What should I focus on next week?

Use your reflections to refine your approach and stay motivated.

Why This Tool Is Effective

- **Action-Oriented**: Transforms results into a clear, personalized improvement plan.

- **Progress Tracking**: Encourages consistency by monitoring daily actions.

- **Flexibility**: Allows adjustments based on what works best for you.

Example of a Filled Improvement Tracker

Date	Focus Area	Action Taken	Success? (Y/N)	Notes/Reflection
Day 1	Prioritization	Listed tasks using the Prioritization Table.	Yes	Helped me focus on the most important tasks.
Day 2	Time-Blocking	Scheduled 2 hours for studying.	No	Got distracted; will try setting a timer.

Blank Filled Improvement Tracker Template

Date	Focus Area	Action Taken	Success? (Y/N)	Notes/Reflection

Date	Focus Area	Action Taken	Success? (Y/N)	Notes/Reflection

Final Tips for Success

1. **Start Small**: Focus on improving one area at a time.

2. **Be Consistent**: Practice daily to form lasting habits.

3. **Stay Positive**: Celebrate small wins to stay motivated.

With your Improvement Tracker, you're equipped to build strong time management habits and unlock your full potential. Keep practicing, reflecting, and adjusting—success is within your reach!

For Parents and Teachers: Key Takeaways from Chapter 32

This final chapter is pivotal in your child's time management journey. The Self-Assessment Results and Improvement Tracker transforms learning into actionable growth. To support your child:

1. Encourage regular self-reflection and honest assessment

2. Help set realistic, measurable goals based on their results

3. Celebrate progress and view setbacks as learning opportunities

4. Model continuous improvement in your own time management

Your role is crucial in developing this essential life skill. By helping your child master time management, you're not just improving their productivity—you're reducing future stress, fostering strategic thinking, and setting them up for success in any field. Remember, even top professionals struggle with this skill; your guidance now is an invaluable gift for your child's future.

Part 5

Reflection and Closing

As you reach the final part of this journey, take a moment to reflect on your learning. Time management is a lifelong skill, and this book will remain a valuable resource for your continuous growth and success.

✸ Bonus Resources ✸

Want more adventures and helpful tools?
Visit **SkillfulAdventures.com** to explore free toolkits
created for kids, parents, and teachers.

You'll find **goal-setting worksheets, planners, affirmations,** and
other resources from the *Skillful Adventures*™ series to
support learning and growth beyond this book.

Author's Note

Dear Adventurer,

🎉 **Congratulations!** You've completed this exciting journey through **Time Management Adventures: A Kid's Guide to Mastering Time (Revised & Extended: Second Edition)**—a skill that will **empower you for life**. But remember, time management isn't just something you learn once—it's an **ongoing adventure** filled with opportunities to grow.

Through this book, you've unlocked powerful strategies—from setting priorities and creating routines to mastering focus and using your time wisely. Whether you're tackling schoolwork, chasing dreams, or making space for fun, these tools will help you navigate your days with **clarity, confidence, and success**.

As you move forward, keep these key lessons in mind:

☑ **Small improvements lead to big results**—every step forward counts.

☑ **Practice makes progress**—be patient and trust the process.

☑ **Use tools, strategies, and worksheets** to sharpen your skills.

☑ **Revisit this book** whenever you need a refresher or motivation.

☑ **Share your knowledge**—help friends, mentor younger kids, and become a leader in time management.

⌛ **Your time is one of your most valuable treasures.** How you use it will shape your future. Keep exploring, keep learning, and most importantly, **keep growing**. Your future self will thank you for every moment of effort you invest today.

🚀 **Wishing you success, balance, and adventure ahead!**

Joy Chacko, PhD

Researcher, Author, Educator, and Strategy Execution Consultant